'Nassau harbour, Paradise Bay. We were steaming straight for the island. I checked the compass and the line of palms. About 600 yards to the shore.

   "Continuous soundings!"

   It was shoaling rapidly. Now or never.

   "Hard-a-port!"

   There was an anguished cough from the wheelhouse — then silence.'

The ship may be bound for romantic places, but for the navigating officer it is no idyll. Comedy, love and near-disaster form the happy blend which makes these real-life stories such an enjoyable read. And the fact that this particular ship, MV *Doulos*, is quite unlike any other.

To Elizabeth, for her wisdom
and strength, and Adrian, without
whom, in a very real sense, little
of this story would have been possible

WORSE THINGS HAPPEN AT SEA!

CLIVE LANGMEAD

A LION PAPERBACK
Tring • Batavia • Sydney

Copyright © 1984 Clive Langmead

Published by
Lion Publishing plc
Sandy Lane West, Oxford, England
ISBN 0 85648 697 3
Lion Publishing Corporation
1705 Hubbard Avenue, Batavia, Illinois 60510, USA
ISBN 0 85648 697 3
Albatross Books Pty Ltd
PO Box 320, Sutherland, NSW 2232, Australia
ISBN 0 86760 567 7

First edition 1984
Reprinted 1984, 1985, 1986, 1988, 1990

British Library Cataloguing in Publication Data

Langmead, Clive
  Worse things happen at sea
  1. Doulos (*Ship*)
  I. Title
  623.8'2432   VM383.D6
  ISBN 0 85648 697 3

Printed in and bound in Great Britain
by Cox and Wyman Ltd, Reading

Author's Introduction

This story is true. As that old military tale *The Deck of Cards* has it: I was there. 'I was that soldier.' I watched it all happen and everything I have written is as close to my memory of these events as I have the skill to relate.

Having said this, I must freely confess that this book is very far from being a sober and objective history of the *Doulos* project. That would demand many more pages than I have had time for and a much grander overview than I have been able to take. *Doulos* has sailed the seas now for a number of years – with her unusual cargo of books, her enthusiastic crew of young people, her dedicated team of officers and leaders. I have not always been there.

Also mine is essentially a sailor's story – a view taken from the navigating bridge, the events featuring in the deck Log, the eye on the sea not the shore. And I am very aware that these events in the day-to-day running of this ocean liner are not really the most important ones.

The impact of *Doulos* (and all she represented) on a port during a visit was invariably much greater than any accidental dent she might have made in the quayside – owing maybe to an over-excited tug boat or mistaken command. But it would be this that stuck in my memory, and rightly so, for it was my duty to deal with such matters. From another's viewpoint the proportion might seem a little strained. Just as a telescope trained on the far horizon reflects an accurate, but rather narrow, picture, so too this book takes the perspective of my own observations, enlarging them in the hope that even this limited view may be valuable in itself.

Tons of books distributed, thousands of interested visitors, powerful ideas exchanged at conferences on board – all these were the very stuff of the project. The ship was a moving, living, base for operations, not an end in itself. Young people from the crew trekking off along desert or jungle roads, leaving the ship far behind, speaking and visiting in fuming cities or remote pastoral villages, deep inland. Driving from sea level to snow line, from the cold, high latitudes to the warm and humid tropics; moving on from country to country, the grand design going forward – lives being changed and human spirits rekindled and redirected. This was the wholeness of the project, in which the ship herself played a part – a full part, but still just a part.

I have not ignored the wider story – how could I? But I have left much of it in the background, as a mountaineer relating a climb talks not of the mountain (that is left to the geographer) but of the inch-by-inch challenge he faced on each crag or overhang as he strove for the summit.

My part in *Doulos* was, in fact, very small. I was there as navigating officer to do a professional job. It was sometimes hard and unpleasant, but I believed in the work then and I still do. Truth, love, faith, hope – these are the goals, the needs, of so many people, and I still find it sad that so few are honestly willing to work and pray to bring them to others. We sailed *Doulos* in order to turn such talk into action.

So, then, here is your spyglass. Welcome aboard!

Contents

1
Landfall

The fiery spear of light that was the herald of the tropical dawn flashed up into the twilight sky on the port bow, throwing into sudden and sharp relief the low black line of land ahead and lending a ruddy tinge to the features of the watchkeepers on the bridge of the MV *Doulos*. Swiftly the boiling red ball hoisted itself into a postcard sky and a gentle breeze, rising with the dawn, slid across the bridgewing and let a cool draught trickle through the open wheel-house door.

Not that the land was any surprise. As officer of the watch, I had identified it some hours earlier from the orange trace on the radar screen. Indeed the ship had been lying dead in the water for the last two, gently drifting about fifteen miles from the northernmost tip; close enough to see the regular flash of a solitary lighthouse, but clear of any passing sea traffic.

Grand Bahama!

The look-out, leaning next to me by the open bridge windows, stirred.

'Serr,' he smiled, half turning towards me and gesturing expansively with his arm at the sunrise, in Latin American style. 'The sun is, ah, risen, yes?'

It was my turn to smile. Throughout the voyage I had made a special point of asking him to remind me of sunrises – it was an easy way for me to check the accuracy of the compass. Normally at this time I was busy shut inside the blacked-out chart-room behind the wheel-house working out my morning star fix. Engrossed, I would miss the vital moment unless reminded. This morning I had no more need of the stars, we could see the land. I could feast on the opening splendour of the day in full, for a change. He knew this, of course, but one always played up to the foibles of this strange British officer.

'We will go inside today, yes?' We did not always berth on arrival.

'Lunch-time, I think, Robbie . . . is what the pilot said.' I nodded to the small radio set on the wooden bulkhead behind, looking, as did so much modern equipment fitted in this sixty-year-old ship, out of place and out of time.

Jose Emmanuel spoke again. This ex-army PT instructor from the Argentine liked to know what was going on.

'Ah, then we have to put down the, ah, an-chor for some times?' He stumbled over the unfamiliar English and nautical terms.

'Well, so it would seem . . . '

I left him enjoying the early morning rays flashing across the sea, snapped a quick bearing with the bridgewing compass repeater and ducked through the night curtain into the dimly lit chart-room to refresh my mind on the contents of the captain's Night Order Book. I glanced down the page:

'At first light proceed to make anchorage at 09.00 hrs. Confirm pilot's intentions at earliest opportunity.'

Commendably brief. Well, we now knew what the pilot intended. Clearly the only thing left to do, since the sun was up, was to get the show on the road.

I flung the curtain to the wheel-house aside with a dramatic gesture. I too could command a Latin style:

'Time,' I roared, 'to get this show on the road!'

The helmsman, who had been quietly enjoying a morning cup of coffee, jerked as though struck and narrowly avoided spraying his last mouthful all over the steering compass.

The 'spare hand' – a Swede with a more phlegmatic temperament – thrust an enquiring head through the port-hole he had been cleaning and Robbie skidded to a halt by the flag locker, having sprinted the length of the port wing.

Gimlet-eyed, I rapped out my orders:

'Robbie! Flags! Here . . !' I pulled them in turn out of the locker. 'Ensign, house flag, this for the Bahamas, this for the pilot, these for us . . . up, up, UP!'

'Si Senhor!' Grinning broadly he staggered off like a

drunken washerwoman with his armful of variously coloured bunting.

'Toni!' I swung round on the choking helmsman. 'Take the wheel, test the steering, both motors, both ways!'

Nervously the little Columbian farmer's son jumped to obey. I made a mental note to be just a little bit less hearty next time. At this time of the morning he obviously wasn't ready for such urgent enthusiasm.

'Sven!' I addressed the port-hole. 'Stow all that gear,' I pointed to the rags and pots on the deck, 'and get some binoculars on. I want a look-out while Robbie's flag waving!'

The gentle Swedish smile widened a little and disappeared through the port-hole, reappearing a moment later at the wheel-house door, with binoculars attached.

'Look-out all round,' I cautioned, more soberly.

I took a quick radar bearing of the coast, spun the finger-wheel for ranging and put the position on the chart. Grabbing the phone I dialled the engine room. Soon a roar of machinery told me the phone had been answered.

'Hey, Wong?' I shouted, not for dramatic reasons now – purely to be heard above the noise.

'Nein, ziss is Helmut!' Ah, I had the fourth engineer on the line.

'Time to wind up the rubber band Helmut!'

'OK, OK, I know it is sunrise up zere, but down here we don't get so excited, hien?'

'Ah Helmut, but it's beautiful. Lovely tropical islands, golden beaches, shimmering sands . . .'

'Ya, ya, I know . . . zat is all I have heard from Francoise for the last week. "Just right for a holiday, Helmut!" she says. "Be with the children," she says . . . '

I laughed. All the wives – there were some twenty or so families on board – and the children too, for that matter, had been very excited when the sudden diversion from the programme – to Nassau – had been announced. The ship director had not had so many family applications for time off for a long time. Indeed, I reflected, my name was on the list, too . . .

'Eighty revs, Helmut,' I concluded.

I replaced the phone and moved to the brass handle of the engine room telegraph that linked the bridge with the engineers below.

A light buzzed on.

'Stand-by.' I swung the handle and the buzzing stopped. They were ready to run.

I walked out to Sven on the bridgewing.

'Anything about?'

He indicated two ships on the horizon and the land ahead.

'Nothing to worry us, then.' I swung the telegraph to 'Slow Ahead'. The buzzing light followed and was silent, but deep down in the bowels of the ship, Helmut and his engineers were throwing the levers and starting the pumps that would jerk the massive eighteen-cylinder marine diesel to life, engage the twelve-foot propeller and thrust our 7,000 ton ex-ocean liner and some 300 crew − still mostly sleeping − towards the distant shoreline fifteen miles ahead.

I moved out onto the bridgewing once more, leaning out over the gleaming white painted side and looking down into the sea, fifty or more feet below. The slight vibration of the hull transmitted itself to my feet and I could see, way down aft at the stern, a thin white trail of foam disturb the blue tranquility of the ocean.

'Hard-a-starboard!' I shouted to the helmsman and listened for the answering cry from within the wheel-house:

'Wheel is, ah, hard to starboard , Serr!' Toni had recovered his equilibrium. Slowly the bow began to swing round, tracking across the distant line of the land. The clicking of the compass repeater confirmed the swing. I noted the heading.

'Steady!'

'Steady!' A pause, then: 'Is, ah, steady now, serr, course one eight zero!'

'Steer one eight five, please.' The bow moved slightly, two clicks from the repeater.

'Steady on one eight five, serr!' A hint of triumph in his voice. He had satisfied his noisy and exacting master. He had done well: he had only learnt to steer in the past five days.

I swung the telegraph once more and when the buzzing ceased the light read 'Full Ahead'. The gentle slopping of the sea against the ship's side that had accompanied the last couple of hours on watch changed to the purposeful swish, swish of the recent days on passage, with white water leaping out from the fore-reaching bow to hiss, protesting, down our flanks before meeting at the stern in the wide white road that was now our wake.

Within minutes the bridge phone rang.

'Bridge, first officer.'

A deep gravelly voice greeted my brisk reply: 'Everything going along just fine up there, Clive?'

'Oh, good morning, sir!' It was the captain.

'Yessir, no problem, sir. Nassau ahead, pilot promises around noon, sir!'

'You seem to have got it all tied up, Clive.' A touch of irony in the voice?

'Well, sir, I mean I . . . ' There was a gentle laugh. 'I'll be up when I've got me a shower.' The phone clicked. The captain was a sailor in the old tradition. He had been in the US Mercantile Marine for nigh on fifty years, man and boy. He had served on all types of ship, in all seven seas, in all types of weather. He had been wrecked, beached (once by a tidal wave), battered in bar-room brawls and withal, working his way up from deck boy to captain. But he was also a man who, midway in his career, had discovered a deep faith in God which had changed him from a brutal leader of the lower deck to a truly gentle man under whom it was an honour and privilege to serve. He had a way of springing surprises too, as I was to discover later.

As we closed the island, with the waving palms and white sandy beaches growing steadily in the frame of the wheel-house windows, beneath our feet the complex organization that made up the life of the ship slowly woke to the new day.

Even at first light there had been a few solitary figures quietly sitting in odd corners of the deck, taking a few moments of quiet and meditation before the rigours of work. Soon these disappeared and more purposeful groups appeared.

First visible to the bridge-watch was a group of deck men and the 'bosun', a tall reedy Irishman with a laconic wit, who with instructions from my immediate boss – the chief officer or 'mate' – began to rig the lifting equipment and derricks that would lower the three heavy gangways into position on arrival, and disembark the ship's 'transport' – some half dozen vans of indeterminate ancestry, faithfully maintained in service by the indefatigable mechanics from the engineers' department.

The mate, as usual, conducted operations at the top of his not inconsiderable voice, accompanied by rapid and violent gesticulations. These were punctuated by howls of frustration or delight, depending on the success or otherwise of the operation in hand. The performance, fully orchestrated in some twelve parts by the deck crew, with bosun on lead shackle, was received with a hearty round of applause from the audience which had assembled on the upper deck balcony, as it reached its resounding and, fortunately, seamanlike conclusion, with both derricks poised and ready for work. The mate and the bosun gravely took a bow from the raised podium on the forward masthouse and led the cast off, stage left, to the fo'c'sle.

But most of the work was not so visible. Deep down in the after hold, below the large sheltered area of deck that housed the book exhibition, staff from the exhibition department were already stripped to the waist and pushing, pulling, lifting and shoving boxes, trays and pallets of books onto the lift which traversed the intermediate decks and cabins to the display area above. Here other labouring workers would unload the books and trundle them on trolleys to the shelves and cabinets now being pulled from their sea-going lashings, washed and polished to receive them.

As each load clanged to deck level a shift supervisor made an entry on his clipboard as to number and contents, while two decks below the stock computer made a similar, electronic note. The information about stock and prices on any one of some 3,000 titles could be required for inspection by the customs officers on arrival. The computer could print out any, or all of the information on demand.

Forward, at the other end of the vessel, the galley, the ship's kitchen, was also hot and busy. At the cooking range the junior cook and his assistant were anxiously piling up gently leaning towers of 'eggy bread', concerned lest the ravenous hoards, expected by the minute, would be ready to destroy their architecture before they had had time to complete it. To their right lay the pyramid of loaves, ammunition for the frying-pan, which was their morning allotment out of the fifty or so baked for use that day. Those which did not suffer the indignity of being submerged in egg had to be stacked in baskets, one for each table. The whine of the slicing-machine mingled uneasily with the fizzle and plop of the hot fat. Further aft another assistant, wielding a soup ladle like the sword of a demented *samurai*, was dividing the contents of a sack of cereal among the fifty or so steel bowls at his elbow. Breakfast was almost ready.

The galley, comprised of bakery, servery, cooking and preparation areas, ran the whole width of the ship. It had to provide nearly one thousand meals a day when the ship was at sea and often many more in port, with visitors and conference guests to be catered for. In a ship where miracles of effort were not unusual, this surely ranked as one of the most unsung and unstinting.

Further forward still lay the sixty or so tables that could seat 400 at one time in the light and airy dining saloon, the second largest and possibly the most attractive room on the ship. The morning's team of servers were receiving a final briefing from the dining supervisor for the day:

' . . . and *don't* forget the hot milk for the families with babies, please!' She concluded her remarks and glanced down at her wrist, noting at the same time that a nonchalant group of staff and crew had gathered outside the locked glass doors at the entrance.

'Better than any watch,' she thought to herself as she

picked up the phone and dialled the information office, way above her head on the lounge deck.

'Breakfast,' she said briefly, when the phone was answered. Almost at once, as though the girl at the information desk was herself keen to eat, the three chimes rang out over the public address system, announcing the meal in all quarters of the ship.

As I heard the tones on the bridge loudspeaker, my imagination drifted down to the small cabin with its annexe and bunk beds for the children that was our family home on board. Inside there would be the minor domestic holocaust that greeted every dawning as Elizabeth, my wife, shocked into wakefulness only minutes earlier by the arrival on her bed of two human thunderbolts, fielded the rain of shirts, shorts, arms, legs and sandals in an attempt to get the wriggling monsters ready for breakfast.

Not that she was alone in her plight. In the other family cabins scattered throughout the hull the same scene would be in rehearsal, in a variety of different tongues and accents. Even when they had reached the tables the wail from hungry young mouths would more than likely drown out the subdued murmur from the remainder of the crew.

But I would not be seeing my family this morning. Relieved of the watch at eight, by the second officer, I would have to grab a quick bite in the working mess, change into my day uniform and return to the bridge for the anchoring.

This thought brought me back to the chart of the anchorage, which I had already laid out on the table in preparation for the captain. It was a large-scale study of the approaches to Nassau harbour, a secluded inlet protected from the sea by a natural island which is long and thin. This island, lying off the coast proper, affords not only protection for the busy berths – Nassau is a much-frequented cruise-liner port – but, on its seaward side, possesses one of the best beaches in the world for swimming: Paradise Bay.

At present, although still a long way off, we were steaming straight for the island and this beautiful beach. I looked closely at the carefully-drawn lines and neat figures.

Berthing, with the help of the local pilot, looked easy; anchoring, decidedly difficult.

For a start, we would have to sail in close to the beach, for there was no room inside the harbour itself to anchor safely, and the sea bed rose from the ocean depths only a few hundred yards off shore. In fact, for the anchor to hook into anything worthwhile I calculated we would have to be no further than 400 yards off the dazzling sands, very close for an ocean liner.

Then there was the little matter of the inshore current and the freshening breeze . . . well, we would just have to steam straight up to the beach and then make a snappy turn into wind and current. Quite an interesting prospect. Still, a neat pirouette just off shore would certainly impress the swimmers and with such short notice for this visit we could do with telling people we were around. The captain wouldn't turn a hair, that was for sure.

My self-consultation was interrupted by the sound of steps on the ladder outside the chart-room door, which opened to reveal the beaming face of the man himself.

'Oh, hello, sir!'

'Clive, I want you to do a favour for me.' I smiled inwardly. Captains, even warm-hearted ones, do not ask favours from first officers. One does what one is told.

'Sir?'

'Could you bring her to anchor for me?'

I stepped back, colliding with the chart table.

'Good experience, you know, Clive.'

'Oh, ah, yes, sir, thank you, sir.' That inward smile had now disappeared completely.

'You go down and get some breakfast with Elizabeth and the boys. I'll hold right on up here till Jeff comes.'

Jeff Linemarker was the second officer due on at eight — ex-US Navy, adding further weight to the American contingent on board. I swallowed again and handed over the watch, pointing out the navigation marks on the looming island. Then I fled below.

The dining saloon was buzzing with excited conversation

about the landfall, punctuated with the normal screams and wails, as I made my way between the tables to the three blond heads of my own family. Timothy, aged eighteen months, squealed with delight on catching sight of me and immediately rammed a soggy spoonful of cereal into his mother's ear to indicate my approach. Richard, the quiet one, grinned briefly and returned to a disinterested study of his untouched plate.

'Hello, love,' I opened.

'You *do not* wave your spoon about like that. Just *look* at my dress. Now *eat!*' she replied, with a nod of greeting.

I dipped into my cereal and briefly explained my unexpected appearance and the captain's, equally unexpected, confidence in my skills. She was unimpressed.

'If you mess it up, we certainly won't get any time off here,' she observed with unerring logic. 'You *will* eat it all up.' she added.

'Very true,' I thought, and, taking the hint, spent the rest of the meal persuading Richard to consume his breakfast. I met with only limited success. He knew I wouldn't throw him to the sharks anyway.

'They probably wouldn't eat me, even if you did,' he pointed out. 'But,' he brightened considerably as a thought struck him, 'they might like my cereal, eh, Dad?'

'Very possibly,' I conceded.

2
Left Hand Down A Bit

The land was close now and we had slowed to manoeuvring speed. The bridge was teeming with life. So too were most of the open decks below, largely in response to the 'pipe' I had just made over the public address system for the crew to report to their anchoring stations.

Everyone knew what that meant. It would be a dollar a minute from here on in and they weren't about to miss any of it. This time, unfortunately, I was to be the star attraction, unbeknown to most of them.

Anyway, the mate was enjoying himself, providing the warm-up for the show. Shouted commands and various windmillings from the fo'c'sle indicated that the anchors were being cleared away and prepared to run out smoothly when the word came. The mate was an expert. There would be no slip-up there, that was certain.

On the bridge with me was Robbie, now back as look-out. The flags he had hoisted were now flying bravely overhead. Toni had been replaced at the wheel by Dane, a very experienced seaman, trained in the Canadian Navy. We would need his quick response and smooth competence when manoeuvring began. There were also the other two deck officers: Jeff, to pass my instructions by walkie-talkie to the chief officer on the fo'c'sle, and Paul Head, the third officer, to take bearings and 'fix' the ship on the chart as we headed in. The final member of the team was Enrico, a Venezuelan, for most of the time the ship's fireman, who had to watch that most vital instrument of all, the echo-sounder. His disembodied shouts, drifting out through the chart-room port-hole, would tell me how much, or how little, water we had under the keel and, more immediately, when the sea bed began to shelve up sharply as we approached the shore.

The captain stood quietly at the back of the open bridge deck, saying nothing.

The brass telegraph handle stood at Slow Ahead. We had reduced speed to the absolute minimum at which we could still steer effectively. It still seemed too fast. An excited babble rose from the spectators on the decks below as they pointed out the rapidly growing features of interest on the sandy shore. Why, I wondered, had they not gone back to work by now? Surely they all had jobs to go to?

'Sounding?' I roared. The opening lines of the drama. From the depths of the chart-room came the reply:

'Nothing, serr! Nothing yet!'

It was on the shallowest setting, so that was reasonable. Paul, the third, spoke quietly:

'Six cables to run.'

Close though. We had just over half a mile to go to my chosen anchoring position – and still no bottom!

The beach was so close now that I could see individuals clearly without binoculars. I looked forward over the bow to the line of palm trees fringing the eastern end. My guide marks. Dane had her rock steady, but the current was carrying her across.

'One seven five!' I ordered.

'Steer course one seven five!' His calm and trained response followed in ritual manner. Then, in a moment:

'Steady on course one seven five, sir!'

I noted my compass and the line of trees. Five degrees had been enough to steady the drift. There was a sudden exclamation from within:

'I have sounding! Twenty-five, no, twenty-four fathom, coming up ver' fast!'

'Twenty-four fathoms, shoaling. Aye, aye,' I acknowledged.

'Five cables.'

'Five cables. Aye, aye.'

My markers told me she was drifting again. The current was picking up, inshore. I glanced at the repeater.

'One six five!'

'Steer course one six five, sir!'

'Steady on course one six five, sir!'

'Very good. Sounding?'

'Fourteen fathoms, serr!' I turned to Jeff.

'Stand by starboard anchor, three shackles in the water.'

He put the radio to his mouth and relayed the selected anchor and length of cable I expected to use to the fo'c'sle. The mate acknowledged with a mutter to the microphone and a wave of the hand.

'All ready for'ad,' relayed Jeff. I nodded. The beach seemed to be surging forward to meet us and I was sorely tempted to stop the engine. But to do so would be to throw away the forward speed I needed to swing the ship round at the last minute. Some of the bathers were waving. The captain held his peace – possibly his breath.

Suddenly there was a clatter on the outside ladder to the bridge and the angular form of the ship director sprang into view. He beamed around warmly.

'Morning Captain, morning Clive, g'morning Jeff, how's it going?' He continued round the available faces. I smiled back through clenched teeth.

'Perfect timing!' I muttered savagely.

'Now see here, Dean,' opened the captain, and drew him into conversation.

'Three cables!' There was a hint of laughter in Paul's soft Irish lilt, and some concern. Three cables. About 600 yards to the shore. We were on the turning-point. I checked on my palm trees and the compass. They looked good. The time had come.

'Continuous soundings!' I ordered. Enrico commenced a monologue of numbers:

'Thirteen, thirteen, twelve 'n haf, twelve, twelve, eleven 'n haf . . .'

It was shoaling rapidly. Now or never.

'Hard-a-port!' I bellowed, taking a leaf out of the mate's book. There was an anguished cough from the wheel-house and then silence. 'Hard-a-port the wheel!' I redoubled my volume. Heads turned round on the decks below.

Still no response, then a vague:

'Er, port . . . ?'

My mind reeled as both the captain and second officer raced for the wheel-house door in a simultaneous bid to wrest the wheel from the clutches of an obviously immobilized helmsman.

A detached observer, aware of the facts, might be excused for finding some touches of humour in the situation that presented itself. Certainly we would not be short of publicity, and free publicity at that, if we ran 7,000 odd tons of ocean liner full tilt up the most popular beach in Grand Bahama. So generous-hearted a man as the ship director might even have been able to view it this way had he not been confronted by the disturbing sight of the most senior officer of the ship, closely followed by his nearest compatriot, apparently engaged in the nautical equivalent of a Le Mans start. Thus alerted to the full dramatic import of the situation he may have been tempted, for a moment, to follow suit. Being, however, a man of great spiritual strength and fortitude he took, in the words of the International Regulations for Prevention of Collision at Sea, 'such action as would best aid to avert collision', and prayed.

It certainly helped, for, unusually for me, my mind moved faster than the captain's feet and, fortunately *Doulos*' keel. Before either of the competitors had reached the door, Light had Dawned.

We had put our best helmsman on the wheel, in order to avoid just this sort of problem. Why? Because he was Navy trained. The Navy, I suddenly remembered, always uses degrees. I had used the Merchant Service order for maximum wheel. Our experienced helmsman had never before heard the expression!

'Port thirty-five!' I bawled at the retreating backs of Jeff and the captain.

'Port thirty-five, sir!' came the relieved reply.

'Thirty-five of port wheel on, sir!'

I offered a fleeting prayer of thanks for the small amount of naval training I had added to my merchant qualifications.

The captain and second officer turned round. The ship director opened his eyes.

Enrico, oblivious, continued his litany of depths:

'Eleven, ten 'n haf, ten 'n haf, ten . . . ' Still shoaling, but by now the palms were sweeping round the bow as we hauled round to port under the effect of maximum rudder, 400 yards from the shore. Close, but we would make it.

'Stop engine!'

We were now lying parallel to the shore.

'Half astern!' We would have to stop properly in the water and even begin to move backwards before I could safely let the anchor go.

'Midships!' The rudder was no more use to us now. Slowly we drew to a stop, the frothing white water of the wake spilling out around the stern and gradually making its way forward, creeping along the side. We had gathered sternway, the current would do the rest.

'Stop engine!' The thudding beneath our feet died away.

'Let go!' This last was addressed to Jeff for transmission to the fo'c'sle, but so loud had my orders become that it carried without need of the radio. The mate certainly approved. There was a splash and rattle of chain cable over the windlass gipsy, and a bloom of rusty smoke.

The anchor dived for the rocky bed. It caught and, as the brake was applied under the mate's careful instructions, held. After a few minutes the radio crackled in Jeff's hand.

'Brought up at three in the water,' he confirmed. We had anchored and could await the pilot safely.

'Kinda warm back there, for a minute, Clive.' The captain paused beside me as he crossed the bridge.

'Had a wheelman die on me once, you know. Can't be too careful.' He turned to follow the ship director down the steps.

'Pilot at noon, eh?'

'Yessir.'

'Keep up the good work.'

'Yessir, thank you, sir.' He disappeared to the bang of his cabin door.

I took a few moments filling in the Deck Log with the incidents of the morning and then strolled outside to find Jeff checking the anchor bearings. He would be keeping the watch at anchor until noon when the pilot would be out to us in his launch. Together we leaned on the rail in companionable silence, slowly unwinding in the morning sun from the tensions of the last hour.

'What is it now, then, three weeks?' Jeff broke the silence and identified my thoughts. The next port would be Florida. It would be my last — for Elizabeth, myself and the boys would all be leaving the ship. Another British officer would be coming out to take my place.

'Humph.' I was half in agreement with his estimate, half avoiding the import of the event. Three or four weeks was now in the realm of 'soon', as against 'next month' or 'whenever we get to the States'. How was I supposed to feel? Joyful? I had certainly claimed to be pleased often enough.

After a long, nine-month voyage we would certainly be happy to be going home. But regrets were creeping in too, now that the end was really in sight. Regret, most naturally, at the anticipated loss, or at least distancing, of so many good friends. They were friends made not from the natural contact of neighbours or shoppers in a town or village, nor from common ground or common interests; naturally speaking, many of us had had little in common. No, these friendships were based on the sort of links that are formed by people, say, evacuated in wartime, or thrown together by natural disaster — unchosen, unexpected friendships forced by circumstances, and forged by shared, often desperate, circumstances. We had come through a lot together, far more, certainly, than I had grown used to on other ships, on more ordinary trades. I would miss them.

I had joined my first shipping company at seventeen as a keen, and green, cadet and had since travelled the world on everything from passenger liners to pilot cutters. Cargo ships, ferries, even warships had had the dubious honour of counting me among their crew. But *Doulos* was different from these.

She was different in obvious ways – her special purpose, her cargo, her unique ship's company drawn from Christian believers of so many different countries. But this was not, or not entirely, the difference that would enrich our memories or lend the depth to our friendships when they were more distant. It was her capacity for the unusual, the unexpected, the bizarre, even. Her ability to turn the most innocent and peaceful voyage – or for that matter, arrival at anchor – into a nautical drama pregnant with suspense, surprise and sometimes danger was worthy of a master novelist or spinner of salty yarns under a swinging lantern.

The challenges we had met as a company were nearly always unforeseen, though not for lack of peering ahead, or seamanlike preparation. But they called for extra effort, imagination; always co-operation, and always humour. These were the things that had determined our friendships, thrown us together in a struggling heap and sorted us out into a working crew. And it was this that would make the parting more difficult, for shared experience is the strongest of all natural bonds, as clubs and 'old boys' associations the world over testify.

I would miss the ship too, simply because of her style. She was very old, but still graceful, and had stood up to our mistakes well, like an ageing princess who is never caught off her guard by the gaucheries of those she meets. *Doulos* was a good sea ship who did as she was told, most of the time. Built in the days when men still feared and respected the sea, she was strong and seaworthy, with no corners cut in her building. Her stem was a solid bar of iron, not the soft plates of modern construction: it had cleaved more than a million miles of ocean. She rattled a bit, but then I expected I would too at sixty-five.

My mind reached back to the time when I had never heard of *Doulos*, or what she stood for, or the hopes and fears for her future. I recalled how we had, inevitably, it seemed, been brought into collision. And collisions, as everyone knows, are what sea stories are often made of.

3

On The Waterfront

'*How* much?!'

My exclamation nearly made the driver of the van in which we were carefully negotiating the steep and narrow streets of the Genoan waterfront drive headlong into the murky waters of the harbour. But I felt I was entitled to my outburst.

Half an hour earlier I had been looking down on these streets and wharves from the cabin window of the morning flight from London, Gatwick, hopefully trying to glimpse the white superstructure of the ship I was about to join there, briefly, as second officer.

As I had understood it from the urgent brief I had been given the previous day at the shipping office in Bromley, I had two days to orientate myself before we put to sea, bound for Bremen, West Germany, where the old liner, until recently laid up, would be refitted and converted into a 'mission ship' for exclusive Christian and educational work in Third World and other countries.

The idea, already tried and tested on a much smaller ship (the *Logos*), was to carry a large stock of books, containing both Christian and educational titles, which would be exhibited for sale in the various ports of call. The ship would be manned and run by volunteers, mostly young people, with an essential sprinkling of experts, all committed to expressing their personal faith in action by working (hard) on board and learning more about themselves and God in the process.

Another important part of the project – and one in which it was hoped that *Doulos* might, with her large lounges and meeting-rooms, prove better equipped than *Logos* – was the conference and teaching work. A free invitation would be issued to any who cared to come along, and advice and help, in the form of seminars, would be offered on everyday problems and situations. Marriage, children, losing a loved one, beliefs and morals – all would be explored in the light of the Bible and the words of Jesus.

It was, on paper at any rate, a grand and exciting attempt by (originally) a small group of dedicated Christians to help others in a practical way and to show God at work in the lives of the crew and the running of an ocean liner. The ship, they said, was in his hands. Just what that meant, I was about to find out.

I had arrived prepared, shortly, to sail. But the information I had just received while bouncing over the cobble-stones of northern Italy put a rather different light on the matter. It seemed that the organization was a little short of money. A low, hollow, laugh echoed round my mind and would have shown in a smile if the seriousness of my plight had not become so suddenly apparent:

As a professional navigating officer I had been prepared to give up three weeks' holiday with my home and family and fly out to take the ship to sea, for free. It was a small Christian service I could perform to help this worthy venture. But if they had run out of money, not only was sailing unlikely, so too was my return air ticket.

My companion repeated the figure needed: five figures, going on six. A staggering sum. He also put it into Italian lire and American dollars, in case I was happier with it that way. I wasn't. The multiplication only made it sound worse. I debated quickly with myself the wisdom of demanding an immediate return to the airport and using some of my own money to fly home. But I realized that I had promised three weeks of my time to these people and their ship. If they were going to let me down, I would not precipitate matters.

The van drew up by a rather grubby and definitely disused wharf front. Disused, that is, for commercial cargo handling – it was full of ships that reminded me of nothing so much as an old folks home. Moored stern on to the quay, in pairs, lay the elderly and rusting hulls of ships waiting, most forlornly, for a prospective second-hand buyer. They were, loosely speaking, in 'good running order'. It was not a scrap yard, but only just. A minimum of light and power kept on, a watchman patrolling the decks – and there they floated, nodding gently to each other and dreaming of times past, ages of elegance and grace when they had been the epitome of modern luxury and speed.

One ship, however, veritably bustled with activity. Her classic clipper stern, hanging out, nearly over the quay itself, proclaimed her name: *Doulos*.

I had arrived.

Despite the foreboding engendered by the conversation in transit, I was pleasantly surprised. I was hailed cheerfully by the total strangers on deck as I strode up the stern gangway onto the poop deck, resplendent with massive (man-high) double steering-wheel, connected direct to the rudder – for emergency steering only, I hoped.

I looked about.

Although the ship was certainly old, it seemed that a lot of good work had been put in to make her properly seaworthy. As I trod the carpeted interior towards the chief steward's office, where I would be allocated my cabin, the bright lights and cheerful decor proclaimed this to be a ship that had had fare-paying cruise passengers on board not many months before. Not long out of service. That was another plus.

My spirits began to rise. I had been trained on passenger ships and knew the ropes on this sort of vessel. The chief steward proved to be a large and ever-smiling Dutchman. He needed to be, to weather the problems of food and accommodation, his 'part of the ship'.

I went forward to my cabin – just under the bridge. Like the crew accommodation on most passenger ships it was small and cramped, but adequate as long as one wished to stay horizontal. I changed into my working clothes and went for a look around.

First stop, the bridge. Entered through the chart-room, the wheel-house presented a picture of wartime period charm – and I don't mean World War II. Hand-cranked telephones, steam steering, brass speaking-trumpets and a large, wooden, magnetic compass centre frame. There were one or two modern additions – fitted in the forties: gyro repeater (still brass) and radio D/F set, with valves. There was also, wonder

28

of wonders, a radar set, its bulk proclaiming its vintage. It was the newest item there.

'Does one raise steam for this, too?' I enquired of the figure I had spotted by the flag locker (containing what, I was tempted to suppose, was the most up-to-date communications equipment on board), nodding at the redolent radar.

'Possibly,' he replied. 'though it's hard work on the arms keeping the scanner going round – lost the key to the clockwork, see.'

He grinned and introduced himself as the officer who had been 'holding the fort' until I arrived. Soon we were engaged in technical discussion from which I gathered that most of the equipment was good and worked ('they don't build 'em like that any more') but needed rather more loving than learning to obtain the best results. I also discovered that I would have something of a free hand up on the bridge, as the captain was leaving shortly.

This time my reaction was muted. Either I had begun to realize that things were a little different on this ship, or I was just stunned.

'We can't sail without a captain,' I ventured cautiously, feeling just a little obvious in my comments. After all, I reflected (in fact mistakenly), the shortage of money could possibly be made up from some quarter of this large organization, but sympathetic Christian captains with free time to spare for this sort of trip hadn't exactly been queueing up outside the shipping office when I'd dropped by yesterday.

'What we have to do,' he said, as though explaining something to a dense child, 'is pray one in.'

There was no answer to that. As an active Christian I believed in the value of prayer – it was important communion with God. But such a direct and urgent request? For a captain? Just like that?

'I suppose,' I replied, light dawning a little, 'that we will be praying in the money, too?'

'It won't come unless we do.'

'No reserves?'

'No.'

'I see.'

'No, you don't. You haven't seen it happen yet. I was here when they bought this ship. That money was prayed for, too.'

'Oh.'

'Look.' He adopted a conciliatory tone. 'If we tell everybody that this operation is run by God, and we believe he wants it operational then we reckon he's going to help us out, given our work and prayers. We've just got to ask him − it's in the Bible: "Ask and you will receive" and so on, you know.'

'Er, yes.'

'Prayer night tonight,' he continued. 'Day of prayer tomorrow. You'll see.'

We locked up the bridge and made our way down to the dining saloon for tea. At the end of the meal, as appeared to be the tradition, I was asked forward to be introduced to the ship's company, along with one or two others who had just arrived. We were greeted with a round of applause. Considering my state of mind, this sort of welcome was the last thing I needed.

Following this, it was confirmed that the captain and my new companion were indeed leaving and that the 'prayer night' would therefore include the request for another captain; plus three carpenters and an electrician for good measure. Also on the agenda to be brought before the Almighty (the name seemed, all of a sudden, to be most appropriate) was the 'financial situation'. We went up to the large main lounge to make a start − with singing.

'Certainly different,' I thought, as reverently as I could.

It was not just a captain and money on the list.

We prayed for generator parts, lubricating oil, shoring timber, welding-rods, flour, paint, canvas, in fact all of the items that the various departments were short of.

We prayed for people − those who had a heavy workload and those who had little, those who were leaving and those who were working ashore on administration.

We prayed for countries near and far and the work of the Christian church there, work often nothing to do with the ship and its anticipated operations, but known to be in need of spiritual support.

We also spent a lot of time thanking God for work already done. It was quite a marathon and ran into the small hours of the morning with ease. It happened like this, I learned, every week.

But if I had expected the deck-head to open up and golden pieces of eight to rain down into our empty coffers I was disappointed. Nor did any new captain stand, smiling hopefully, at the head of the gangway when we went, eventually, to bed. Nothing strange or unusual seemed to have happened at all. Indeed the people praying were themselves very ordinary: young people, from many different countries, dressed in the main in jeans and sweaters, sitting quietly in groups, expressing their confidence in God and their concern that he should help in the practical areas of their lives. It seemed to me altogether too honest and too simple. I remembered that the early church was full of simple people, too. Or were they just simple-minded?

The next morning I was introduced to the 'deck department', the group of officers and sailors (only one of the latter was a professional) who ran the ship from a seamanship and maintenance point of view. My department. As navigating officer I would not be working alongside them very much. My place was the bridge, preparing the charts and instruments for the voyage – but it was good to feel part of the ship's company proper and to meet the mate.

We said a short prayer and set to work, having been reminded that our allotted hour for the day of prayer was just after lunch. Each department took an hour out of the day, one after the other, providing a sort of chain but without disrupting the work of the ship too much.

I repaired to the bridge, and the officer shortly to depart formally handed over the running of the navigation, and left me to it. There was a lot to pick up and, as I got to grips with the work, I found myself gently dropping the odd hint to God about the state of a chart or the error in an instrument . . .

The two days passed very quickly. There was a great deal to do and only me to do it. With no captain in residence and the mate busy on deck I had to take decisions myself which would normally have been taken for me. But things fell into place with surprising ease. Even the chronometer seemed to tick with a godly enthusiasm, and experiments proved my predecessor right: the equipment did work, in the main, even the radar (which needed neither steam nor clockwork in the event), but always at a leisurely pace. People had more time in those days.

But still: no captain and no money.

Day three came and went. The sailing was delayed – not that many people were unhappy about that. I, for one, was still repairing and refurbishing much of the equipment – all the compass repeaters had had minor faults, not to mention the steering gear, which was leaking steam, and therefore pressure, everywhere. It made the steering-room at the stern, along with the aft mooring position, like a sauna bath when the rudder was put over. A messy afternoon repacking the valves with the third engineer solved that one, though it still got a bit foggy down aft at full rudder . . .

Day four was designated another day of prayer and I marvelled at the enthusiasm with which the ship director led the ship's company through their various meetings. My own faith was wearing just a little thin, and the fears that had risen so urgently on my first day aboard were stirring again. Still, at least by the afternoon I was ready for sea, gear repaired, charts up-to-date, gyro compass running and stable. It seemed that the engineers were happier too: number two alternator, for instance, had consented to work normally again after a bearing change. (Mind you, it had been the object of so much prayer recently, I was surprised that it hadn't been requisitioned as stand-by in heaven.)

An air of expectancy had gripped the ship. Everywhere I went, on or below decks, the question in conversation was the same:

'Has it come?'

'No.'

'What about a captain?'

'No.'

'What is He waiting for?'

I wasn't sure.

At tea that evening, the ship director stood up with a solemn expression on his craggy features. He beckoned to a diminutive man who came hesitantly to the front.

'Allow me to introduce,' he intoned, his eyes sparkling just a little, 'Captain James Sand, retired commodore of the British Shipping Company . . . '

He continued with the introduction. I was thunderstruck. By coincidence I had heard that a deeply-committed Christian captain had recently retired from a famous shipping company, as senior master (commodore), and I had particularly wanted to meet him. I had certainly not expected such a time or place!

Commodore Sand briefly told the strange tale of the regular daily Bible verse that had seemed to leap at him from the page the day before – 'Offer your willing service to God' – the restless night that followed, and the telephone call from a distant colleague that had made him aware of the need on *Doulos*. He had caught the first flight to Genoa.

The ship director continued.

'I had a telephone call from the European co-ordinating office this afternoon, in Belgium. They had a cable today. It reads: "Gifts totalling (here he read out a six-figure sum) now to hand from bank transfer, donors anonymous by request, signed International Co-ordinator, England." ' He paused. 'Well what do you think of that?'

The saloon erupted.

There was a time of thanksgiving to God arranged for after the meal, but I didn't go. Instead I went out onto the privacy of the boat deck. The lights of the city looked down and twinkled on the quiet waterfront, and the stars that would now be my guide for the next few days hung close in the still air.

'Well, Lord,' I whispered to no one in particular. 'You've certainly done it this time.' The stars and lights blurred a little.

I made my way forward to the captain's cabin.

4

Fitting Out — Fitting In

Elizabeth is a very beautiful woman, so it's a double tragedy to me when she mars her face with tears — and there were tears now, floods of them. It was three months since I had left the ship, now safe in her refitting berth in a quiet backwater of Bremen to return to England and my family.

Before leaving, I had been asked to visit the ship director in his office. He closed the door, always a bad sign, and then asked me if I would consider serving for a longer period as navigator.

I appreciate blunt people. Not sure if I was being favoured or fooled (couldn't they find anyone else?), I promised to think it over and consult Elizabeth. One of the strict rules of the ship was that families must stay together — which meant that if it was a good thing for me to rejoin, Elizabeth and baby Richard would have to come along as well.

I wasn't sure which was worse: going away to sea and leaving my family behind or bringing them along too — and asking them to make a home on the ship! Neither was Elizabeth. For her it would mean giving up her home. The one we were living in 'went with the job' to which I had returned from Germany. All our furniture and personal belongings would have to be packed up and stored and we would have to make our new home in two small cabins, on a ship that was constantly moving on to somewhere different and new. Nautical nomads. Our address would become just a box number in England, our front door a steel gangway and our neighbourhood, dockland, in different languages. Not a glowing prospect for a young mother with a tiny baby.

We talked it over endlessly.

We believed deeply in the projected ideas for the ship — which was going to provide real help in parts of the Third World, and a training programme on board for the young people. One ship was already in operation, and we had known for some time of the value and effectiveness of the work it had achieved, mainly in India and south-east Asia.

Doulos was intended for South, or more generally Latin, America, where the Christian church is growing at a staggering rate, but is very short of good teaching literature, even Bibles. The large book exhibition could readily meet this need. Conference facilities, too, for Christian ministers and leaders, are almost unheard of or are too expensive. *Doulos'* main lounge, seating 600 and provided free of charge, could literally become a Godsend.

Last, and perhaps closest to our hearts, was the programme of on-board training, for we had already both been involved in a great deal of youth work and knew the need for challenge, learning, mixing and maturing. The largest part of the crew was made up of young people who 'signed on' for twelve or twenty-four months. Never having seen a ship before, nor, in all probability, any other country but their own, they came at their personal expense to offer themselves to help in whatever way the ship director and his staff thought best. They ran the ship under the watchful eye of the leaders and 'experts' (which would include us, if we decided to join) and spent time learning to live together, work together – on some mammoth (and messy) tasks – and study together, for there was also a detailed seminar programme. They had, as someone put it, to roll out of their bunks and hit the ground running, just to keep up! Certainly in Latin America we knew that there would be many who would leap at the chance of such an opportunity.

In all, it was a bold experiment, and they needed our help. But did we want to be a part of it? There was also one other drawback: there would be no pay. As a volunteer I had started, and as volunteers we would have to return. No one else on the ship received any salary, but that didn't make it any easier for us. We wouldn't be embarking on any pleasure cruise, that was for sure.

Still, there was no question about our willingness to serve God – we each had certificates, with the ink barely dry, from two years' brain-tingling effort at Bible College to prove it. But this was not quite the gentle step into 'worthwhile service' that we'd had in mind. The sea was my trade, a way of earning a living. Serving God afloat had never entered my head. Elizabeth had never been keen on 'boats' at all. But God did seem to be making an open request. Was it not our plain duty, as Christians, to obey?

We decided to go – at least until the ship was a proper, going concern. A six-month shake-down cruise was planned, in European waters, before crossing the Atlantic. We could, at least, try that. I telephoned the shipping office. They were delighted – we were committed. Then came the tears. It was only to be expected, and all I could do was love and comfort Elizabeth – and admire her courage. As I held her, they gradually subsided and I suddenly realized that they would not be the last in this adventure – from either of us.

It was only a matter of weeks later that we found ourselves seated in a van similar to the one I had so uncertainly ridden in Italy, but this time speeding down the autobahn from Bremerhaven to Bremen, having crossed on the night ferry from Harwich. Around us lay the twelve items of luggage which seemed to us the minimum required for survival on board, plus baby Richard, who was enjoying himself immensely, beaming at the cars.

Doulos didn't really look her best, in rust and red lead paint, as we rounded the final dock wall to her berth and Elizabeth beheld her for the first time. She narrowed her eyes.

'It doesn't look very big,' she commented briefly. 'But it looks quite friendly,' she concluded, on a positive note. We struggled aboard, with the help of willing hands.

Elizabeth was right, of course. *Doulos* isn't large compared to many passenger ships, but she used to be licensed to carry over 600 voyagers, plus a full crew. Three hundred was our anticipated total complement, so we might have been expected to rattle about a bit inside, except that we were staying months, not days, and that family homes, even in cabins, need more space than holiday ones.

Our cabin was small, but at least we had a separate one next door for Richard, and it was light and airy, with large portholes. Some had none at all. Elizabeth shuddered at the thought. We shared washing and toilet facilities with the third officer, his family and two single engineers, which did cause a problem at times, especially when it came to sorting out nappies. But the third officer, an amiable Belgian, assured us that we were well off compared with the crew of the other ship, who apparently shared facilities with twelve or more, so we held our peace.

With Richard a baby, Elizabeth was soon accepted into the group of wives and mothers. She discovered that they all shared similar problems about leaving the homes and security they had known. Some seemed to cope with the unusual circumstances more easily than others, but although some families had actually spent a number of years in this sort of life (they had transferred from the other ship) it still needed a special measure of grace, patience and tolerance to live and raise a family in a floating, moving home.

But we weren't moving yet. We had joined about half-way through the projected refit time and it seemed as though nothing had been done. Much had, of course, even the paintwork showed that, but there seemed such a mountain left that I despaired of ever seeing it completed. Everywhere the decks were piled high with mysterious items, of no fixed abode. Some apparently, were brand new and ready for installation, others were just so much junk, ready for disposal. Around each there was always a group of intense, and usually dirty, individuals chatting knowledgeably and volubly, and just about to shift it to another part of the deck. Refits never change.

Down below, the carpets were hidden from sight, wisely covered by protective rolls of paper against the endless tramp of booted feet, and the cabin spaces echoed with the bang of hammer, hiss of welding torch and the splintering of wood partitions as a number of the larger ones were turned into the offices needed for the ship's new role. Unlike most ships she had to be self-sufficient in organization and administration, for there was no gleaming company headquarters to refer back to or depend upon. Office space was essential.

To save cost, most of the jobs were tackled by the crew,

augmented by willing volunteers from the local Christian communities and churches. Christian businessmen gave advice and often obtained special prices for equipment and fittings. Other people too, sympathetic to our aims, gave and helped in very many ways. We could have made no progress without such help and goodwill.

Food was another item on which cost was saved. It was horrible. That is not to say that it was bad or unpalatable. I have just been spoilt, ashore by Elizabeth, who certainly knows the way to my heart, and afloat by the luxury cuisine of so many first-class liners. The chief steward would take anything he could get that was good for us and tell the galley to serve it up as tastefully as possible. But somehow my expectations always seemed just that little bit higher . . .

If Elizabeth had sacrificed her home to serve on *Doulos*, I always felt that I had sacrificed my stomach − and it kept on reminding me. Very resourceful too, the cooks. Our first lunch was a good example.

'Oh, it looks like soup!' Elizabeth held up the jug and peered into it. 'It's a funny colour, though,' she added doubtfully.

'Well, pour some out, darling, and I'll pop upstairs and get the microscope.'

'You try it,' she said firmly and thrust the steaming jug across the table. I did. It tasted sweet and vaguely familiar.

'What are those long, funny, stringy bits, Clive?'

'Hmm. It looks like rhubarb, tastes like rhubarb and by golly . . .'

'Rhubarb soup?! You must be mad!' But I wasn't. Not then, anyway. It seemed that the ship had been given several tons of the crop and we weren't going to waste any of it. By the end of the week we had all begun to turn a little red and stringy ourselves . . .

Still, at around 1,000 meals a day, one could understand the need for care and economy, especially if we were shortly to be working in the poorer countries of the world. Despite my opinion of the fare, it wasn't long before one of the ladies on board started a class of 'Weight Watchers Anonymous' (but we all knew who went). I never felt the need to join.

All over our new home, people were chipping and welding, painting and fixing. Inside, a complete phone system was installed with an automatic exchange. Initially I was very pleased. I was sure it would save me a lot of leg work, but gradually I began to change my mind. I found that, because I could be called, I was 'on call' most of the time. Although invaluable, it became less of a blessing.

Power lines were run through by the electricians, toilets were cleared by the plumbers, cupboards and beds were remade and repaired by the carpenters. There seemed to be no part of the ship one could go to without, a minute later someone coming along with an, 'Excuse me, I've just got to fit this up here . . . would you mind . . .'

I spent the greater part of my working day on the bridge. Much of what I had patched up for the voyage north now needed proper repair. Some of the work I could do myself, some needed expert advice, and usually assistance, from the radio officer or the technicians in the electronic control room – a sort of combined recording studio and workshop.

It was good to be able to pick up the (new) phone and find cheerful help waiting on the other end, even when the helper could manage only a few words of English. At least the electrons didn't find the language a problem.

English was the 'standard' language on board. It was the Americans who found it the most difficult to learn. Elizabeth and I did our best to help but, well, you can't win them all. More interesting still was the sort of conversation sometimes overheard between say, a Swiss electrician and a Malay engineer discussing a piece of Italian equipment, in English, for the benefit of a German fitter. I won't attempt to describe it, but you can imagine that there was a lesson in patience being given there somewhere.

The weeks flew by and commissioning day arrrived. Many hundreds of invited guests thronged the main lounge. Crew members were asked to keep clear if not involved (it was a day for our many shore supporters, really), so we did – well clear, taking Richard and pushchair into Bremen town, which, despite being part of a port, we found delightful. Especially the 'old quarter', where small 200-year-old cottages and shops huddle together around cobbled squares and lean towards you as you approach. Prettily painted and preserved, and offering a special line in multi-coloured ice cream (appreciated by two grown-up 'Kinder' and one real one), they recall the traditions and rosy warmth of the old Germany, perhaps by-passed by the success of the modern state.

Meantime, back at base, or perhaps berth, the speeches were made, the vision shared and the intentions blessed, the whole thing being rounded off with prayers and German sausage. We returned just in time for the sausage.

But, commissioning or no, sailing day was the target date for most of us and now that was just one week away. Joined by another officer we at last had a full team on deck and most of the major jobs were completed, except one: the Book Exhibition awning.

This was a rigid structure of wood and steel, designed by the ship's naval architect (yes, we even had one of those) which was being erected over the open after-boat-deck. Covered, this deck would offer nearly 4,000 square feet of deck space on which the presentation cabinets and tables for the books could be placed in shelter and safety. There were about ten more days of work to do, which would overrun our planned departure. I wondered, would the sailing be delayed? For we also had another problem: once again we were short of money.

The whole situation had something of a *dejà vu* feel about it. I had been there before. This time there were more eyes upon us: many in the shipping fraternity who had no time for our hopes and intentions were watching closely. Many had openly scoffed at our beliefs. There were churches who had, voluntarily, pledged quite large sums to the venture. They were watching and had perhaps begun to wonder if we were playing foolish games with their careful offerings.

But the essence was the same: could our prayers touch the generous heart of God? Was he there and was he interested?

As the week closed, two days of prayer were instituted,

following the normal prayer night. Some money was given, though no word of our plight was released from the tight circle of the ship's community; but it was nothing like enough to pay our bills. The sailing was delayed, initially for two days, then for two more.

Some laughed, mouthing 'I told you so' from the security of their carpeted offices, for German businessmen are not fools when it comes to money. Others were fighting to hold on to the vision they were sure they had received from God; and all the while the shipwright and his assistants on deck laboured to complete the awning.

On the fourth day one of the many firms that had helped us so much arrived to finish their work on the rubber compound roof sealant. They were a highly specialized firm and gave their services free of charge. The work was completed. The awning was ready.

That night the last of several large and unexpected sums of money that had been unaccountably arriving throughout the day, from differing sources, was handed in at the Information Desk on board. We had enough to go.

Late, but with all vital work completed, *Doulos* slipped her moorings the following afternoon from the now not-so-quiet river backwater. The quayside echoed to the cheers of the crowd of friends that had gathered, and to the lively strains of a hymn, played by a church band. All assembled especially to wish us God-speed and a safe voyage.

The radio crackled in my hand as I stood by the warping capstan at the after mooring station.

'Let go aft!'

'Let go aft. Aye aye!' The last ropes splashed into the water and the tug took up the strain, pulling us gently clear of the berth.

'All gone aft!' The dripping ropes splashed up through the fairlead onto the deck, to be grasped and coiled down in their bins.

'All clear aft!'

A slight wash kicked up under the counter, swirling the dock water aside in miniature whirlpools. We were under way! Who knew now what adventures lay ahead? Or how many sea miles would race eagerly under our sturdy keel as we voyaged out on our new mission around the world?

Only God – and he wasn't saying.

5

Mercy Dash

I could see that something was up. There was a close huddle in the corner of the main lounge: doctor, ship director and chief officer. It was sending me all the wrong vibrations. So were the expressions on their faces. But whatever the problem was, it had chosen a singularly inappropriate time to surface, as we were in the middle of a party, well, a stage revue actually.

At sea, everyone was taking the opportunity to relax after the efforts of refit except, of course, the watchkeepers (who never omitted to mention the fact, given the chance) and we had all crowded into the main lounge after supper for an evening of jokes and skits, mainly at the expense of the leaders on board. The old band platform in the middle of the floor, left over from the ship's cruising days, was declared the stage and the audience found themselves some deck space around it, on chairs or carpet as they chose.

The evening had gone well, though one of the things we had all discovered was that humour can vary widely around the globe. We had suffered interminably through the tortuous twists and turns of an Asian shaggy dog story involving ping-pong balls, which had kept everyone east of India in stitches, but had largely been lost on the rest of us.

Not to worry, Elizabeth and I were about to redress the balance. We had begged and borrowed (certainly not stolen) the brightest, gaudiest and most mismatched set of clothes we could find on board, including a pair of hats that would have won prizes at the Chelsea flower show. We then armed ourselves with assorted pairs of sunglasses, cameras, lenses and light meters and staggered centre stage.

'Hey there, Honey Lamb, Honey Doll, Honey Pie, Honey Child!' I roared to Elizabeth, thrusting out my stomach, which had been amply fortified by a couple of the chief steward's spare pillows.

'Yees, Elmer, my sweet?' whined Elizabeth, giving me a violently winning smile.

'What is they-at cute li'l ol' bridge over there?'

'Why, they-at's London Bridge, Elmer honey.'

'I just gotta have they-at bridge for my back yard, I just gotta . . .'

I have to record that most of the rest of the transaction was drowned in the roars of laughter that followed. By the conclusion, we had agreed to the purchase of two bridges, the Tower of London and Victoria Station, with the Houses of Parliament thrown in for good measure. Everyone loved it. We had evidently mined a rich vein of international humour, the universal clown. I must hasten to add that the nation that had been the butt of the joke seemed to enjoy it the most.

We ambled off stage, shedding sunglasses and hats in our wake, followed by thunderous applause. But any thoughts of giving up the sea to pursue a career in show business were soon stilled by the earnest concern expressed on the faces of the little group I had noticed a moment earlier in the corner of the lounge. The chief officer glanced up and caught my eye, and I sidled around the back of the audience, now intent on a new act.

'Clive, we've got a problem.'

'Yes, siree?' I was still a little stage-struck.

'Alisa, the shipwright's wife, has gone into premature labour.'

My eyes widened and the humour evaporated like steam from a hot iron. Alisa, a small, quiet, slip of a girl, was six or seven months pregnant, certainly nowhere near her time. Immediately a picture of her came into my mind. I had noticed her on sailing day, her face pinched and white, standing on the upper deck with her husband, who had spent so much extra time on the awning over the last few weeks. Her grimace of fear, as she had pressed into his side, the ship slowly sliding away from the quay, had spoken volumes.

Had her obvious fear of the sea, the unknown, caused her

body to start labour at such an early, and clearly dangerous, stage? I couldn't possibly tell, but with a shock I realized that what to me was an enjoyable and comfortable experience – a sea voyage – was to others something to be feared and dreaded . . .

'We need to divert . . .' The mate broke in on my thoughts.

'Yes, yes, of course . . .' I recovered my mind with an effort and plugged in that semi-conscious mini-computer that all ship's navigators seem to have in their brains, which keeps a constant record of the ship's approximate position, no matter how far away they are from the chart-room.

'How long have we got?' I snapped at the doctor, angry with myself for letting my mind wander so far at the shock of the news. Action was what was needed now, not reflection.

The doctor thought out loud:

'Well, the labour must be stopped before the . . . and then this is her first confinement, so that could be . . .'

'Doctor!' I cut across the detailed evaluation. 'We have to find a port which will take us, get to it, get into it, get Alisa ashore, into an ambulance, then to hospital . . . *How much time?*' I laboured the final words heavily with impatience.

'About two to three hours.'

'No chance of you dealing with her here?' I knew the ship's hospital was small but adequately equipped for some emergencies.

'I've already explained . . .'

I excused myself and left the sentence, and speaker, dangling in mid-air. As I raced along the corridors and up the ladders towards the bridge, the chart of the sea area around us flashed up in my mind's eye. A cross appeared at the ship's position. Mentally I drew an arc around it, with a two hour radius at maximum speed. Thankfully several ports appeared possible. I ticked off the options one by one.

'Dover!' I gasped, as I threw open the chart-room door at the end of my climb, to find the captain bent over the chart table. I looked down at the tip of the pencil he was holding in his hand. A light line already encircled Dover on the chart.

We made a curious pair as we bent over it together. I, gaudily

45

dressed in my American tourist outfit and he, his hair shiny with water, in his dressing-gown. He had been taking a bath when the doctor called.

The ship had made good progress and the series of crosses that marked her track showed that she was nearer the Dover Straits than I had guessed. Something in our favour at least. There was also something else: I knew the harbour well, having served on a number of cross-channel ferries, and could pinpoint the fastest and safest approach.

As we talked over the plan it became clear, too, that we would save a lot of precious time if we did not actually enter the harbour at all, but 'lay off', just outside, by one of the two entrances, and called for a boat. The weather conditions weren't exactly ideal, but safe enough for the short dash a harbour launch would have to make to reach us. Some comfort might have to be sacrificed, but time lost would almost certainly mean the life of the unborn child.

Once clear of us a launch could make straight for the nearest jetty and a waiting ambulance. It seemed the best plan. It would mean taking *Doulos* very close to the harbour wall and then turning to provide some shelter for the boat, but the captain accepted that without question.

I looked at my watch. Just one hour to go.

'Excuse me, sir. I'd better go and change.' The captain nodded and felt his own damp hair.

'Yes, something warm, I think,' he said reflectively. Some minutes later I returned, to find both mate and captain back on the bridge. The mate indicated that he had made the preparations for the accommodation ladder to be ready. This would be lowered down the ship's side at the approach of the launch and provide a stairway from our high main deck down to the smaller craft. Although firmly lashed and held it would prove anything but a steady platform for the transfer. Appropriately, at this point in my thoughts, the captain motioned us into the chart-room once again.

'I think,' he said softly, his solemn features unnaturally ruddy in the glow of the night lighting, 'we should pray, briefly.'

We nodded our assent and, to the accompaniment of the call of the look-out and the answer of the watch officer, the creak of the wheel and the whine of the radar, we each made a short appeal to God for the blessing we knew we needed, thinking particularly of the pale young woman racked in periodic agony several decks below.

We did not know what would happen. We did not know if the God in whom we all set our trust would choose to take her life, or the life of her child. We did not know if the risks we were about to take, mitigated though these were by the experience of our captain, would be justified by events. The faith we held was not that God would do what seemed best to us, but what *was* for the best.

We opened our eyes with the conviction that he would.

'Sandette Bank! 'bout twenty minutes to run!' The curtain parted and the third officer stepped into the chart-room. Muttering figures to himself, the bearings he had just taken, he skilfully drew the lines in on the chart. The captain looked over and grunted.

'Tell the chief fifteen,' he ordered. I called the engine room and warned them that the engine should be ready to manoeuvre in a quarter of an hour. I also told them why. They would be ready.

I followed the captain outside. Over on the starboard bow lay the lights of Dover, as I had seen them so often from the bridge of a homeward-bound ferry. A mass of different colours near the docks, the yellow street-lights of the town and, high on the hill, the floodlit keep of Dover Castle, which for so many years had guarded England's European gateway.

It looked solid and sure, the lights welcoming. I pulled up the hood of my duffle coat against the blast of wind over the dodger and took a bearing. Quietly I pointed out the lights and landmarks for the captain to watch on his approach. He listened and then turned to the parka'd figure of the third officer beside us.

'OK, I'll take her now.' The ship was now under his direct control. The bridge VHF radio crackled:

'*Doulos* this is Dover harbour control.' I unclipped the handset.

'Harbour control – *Doulos*.' Quickly and efficiently the duty controller, alerted by an earlier call, gave us the approach information and assured us of the waiting boat and ambulance. I replied with our thanks and present position.

Dover harbour is one of the busiest in Europe and our imminent intention to block one of the two entrances meant that Hovercraft, ferries, coasters, tugs and fishing-boats due to enter or leave in the next half hour or so would all have to be routed through the one remaining entrance. Listening, I could hear him redirecting the traffic around us, for all the world like an air traffic controller bringing down a damaged aeroplane into a busy airport. They were doing all they could for us, that was evident.

We closed the western end of the harbour from seaward, making out, amidst the blaze of lights, the black stretch of water that was the entrance itself.

'Slow Ahead.' The indicator lights on the telegraph flashed upwards.

'Range, please.' The third officer, his face in the radar hood, sang out the closing distance to the harbour mole.

'Five cables (half a mile) . . . four cables, four . . . three and a half.'

'Stop engine!' The lights flashed vertical and the drumming beneath our feet was stilled.

'Two and a half . . . two . . .' The mole was big and dangerous. Surely we would go no closer.

'Slow Astern!' The engine drummed once again and the captain stopped us dead. *Doulos* lay still in the water, as close to land as we dared.

Two lights appeared in the blackness of the entrance.

'Boat ahoy, sir!' I called out over my shoulder and, grasping the megaphone, leant over the side.

'Lower the ladder! Boat coming through the heads!'

A wave from way below showed me that the mate had heard and in an instant the whole side of the ship was bathed in lights, hitherto switched off so as not to distract the captain on his approach.

Slowly the length of steps crept down the ship's side. I could see the boat clearly now, dancing and leaping in the choppy sea outside the calmer waters of the harbour. A sheet of spray swept across the cockpit. I shuddered and wondered momentarily about the wisdom of our decision.

Quickly, however, the boat drew into our lee, where the water was calmer, protected from the wind by the bulk of the drifting ship. It slid alongside.

Then three figures, one bent almost double, crept slowly down the slanting steps, hesitated at the bouncing boat for what seemed a lifetime and then stepped in. Immediately the boat pushed off and drove clear, making its dash for the smoother waters inside the protective mole.

'Boat away!' For a moment the captain did nothing, his raised binoculars intent on the vanishing boat. Just beyond it, on the quay, the regular flash of a blue light indicated its urgent destination. He lowered them from his eyes.

'Full Ahead!' He looked at the mole.

'A good cable and a half!' He permitted himself a little smile. 'Best not stop around though.'

We put the harbour lights rapidly behind us and headed for the safety and sea-room of the English Channel.

We heard a few days later that, although close, we had been in time and the labour had been temporarily delayed. A few weeks later we also heard that Alisa had delivered her baby safely at the right time. We thanked God heartily for his help and blessing.

But the whole incident had given me much food for thought. I was sure that Alisa's reaction to the ship and the sea had been a product as much of the childish humour amongst the crew (which I had done nothing to discourage) about rough seas, sickness, and the like, as of her own nervousness. It may have been funny to them, but it was not to her, or possibly to many others, particularly the women, who had no experience with which to counter it. Surely it was up to me – and indeed all of the professional seamen on board – to go out of our way to instil confidence in the ship and explain the mysteries of the sea to those to whom it was all so strange and frightening? I felt, somehow, I had a measure of responsibility for the night's events.

Quietly I made a resolution: in future I would wear full uniform when on duty, for that inspired confidence. I would make regular navigational announcements from the bridge, for people fear largely when they do not know. And I would personally supervise the boat and safety parties when they mustered and drilled.

I kept my self-promise. I know this was appreciated, by many; by others it was misunderstood as a 'stuffed shirt' mentality. Maybe they were right, but then perhaps they had not had the opportunity, late one blustery Channel night, to stand by an anxious captain and watch the pain-racked figure of a terrified mother-to-be climb down a narrow swaying ladder to a bucking, spray-drenched boat, driven to it by an unassuaged fear of the sea.

6
Junkyard Bargains

We stood idly by the boat deck rail and watched the sunset. Elizabeth stood close beside me and looked in silence as the heavy disk flashed green and disappeared below the taut line of the far horizon. The clouds were rich with scarlet and gold. It was a moving and romantic moment.

'What are you thinking?' She asked softly, brushing her lips against my ear as she spoke.

'Ah, well, if you must know: charts, flags and azimuth rings, actually.'

'What?!'

'Yes, we're a bit short of all of them and I don't know how . . .' I ducked smartly to avoid the scything blow of her famed tennis forehand, thankfully minus racquet, and was forced to raise my voice considerably to hail the rapidly diminishing figure.

'Hey, look, I'm sorry . . ' The figure disappeared into a doorway, to the thump of a solid teak weather door.

'Humpf!' I consulted the lifebuoy on the bulkhead beside me. 'Women!' I gazed woefully out to sea; the grey Atlantic horizon looked back. 'Women and ships don't mix,' I concluded sagely. 'Not really their fault.'

I realized that seamen have a deep understanding of these things. Still, there was no doubt it was going to prove a problem. The charts, flags and azimuth rings, that is.

When we had commissioned, we had only been able to buy enough charts for our short 'shake-down' cruise. They are not cheap and a full set can cost many hundreds of pounds. Pounds that, in this case, had already been earmarked for more pressing needs. After all, our Atlantic crossing was six months or so away and charts to cover that, and the whole of South America, could be bought later. But I would have liked them on board, even if just to get them sorted and catalogued for our purposes, as well as corrected up-to-date.

Then there were the flags. We had one, old, complete set. We had to. It was a sound, legal requirement. But, really, they were all mostly on their last legs – or threads. I'd have given them six months, as long as it wasn't windy. Anything over force four and our signal hoist would begin to look like washday in down-town Naples. Not a pretty sight. A few spares – of the more commonly-used ones would come in handy, too. Share the load, so to speak.

Normally, with any shortage of this kind I would fill out an order to the company and send it off through the shipping office. But *Doulos* didn't work like that. And as for the azimuth rings, well, what could be said?

An azimuth ring is a brass, fitted ring which drops over a compass or compass repeater. On *Doulos*, as on most ships, we had a repeater on each bridgewing. Each required its own ring. On the ring, various sights and mirrors are mounted to enable the hopeful officer on watch to make an even stab at the compass bearing of, say, a lighthouse, or an approaching ship. It's something that one uses all the time, in fact. An essential tool.

Ours were rotten. Manufactured in 1942 – I know because it was stamped on them – they gave every indication that they had been used on a submarine of the same vintage and left up top every time it went under water. Warped and twisted, with wire sight hairs that fell onto the compass bowl when looked through, our two azimuth rings returned navigation to the adventure it had been several hundred years ago. After use, one always felt a warm glow of achievement if two out of the three bearings taken came anywhere near the expected position of the vessel. In short they were a menace to the safe navigation of the seas and would have to go. (The third officer, by the way, loved them and got a perfect fix every time.)

As for replacement, again cost was the problem. The precision instruments they should have been certainly fetched a fine price in the catalogues. Outvoted by the rest of us he may have been, but the third officer, it seemed, could rest secure in the knowledge that he would be using his rings for some time to come.

I consulted with the captain. I consulted with the ship director. More significantly I consulted with the finance officer, a delightful German with a dry sense of humour and a firm answer: No. At least, not yet.

'You should get down to some praying, Clive, The Heavenly Ship Chandler. Maybe he is waiting to file your order.'

It was the obvious answer. But, then, I had spent many years on other ships where it would have been very far from what was expected. My experience was the reason why I was on board, but that experience had not generally included praying for deficient items of bridge equipment. I knew by now that God could run the ship as a whole – but *my* half-hearted requests – would they be entertained?

All the same, I did add charts, flags and azimuth rings, a little shyly, to my rather infrequent prayers.

Our next port of call was Bilbao in northern Spain. On passage through the Bay of Biscay we heard to our chagrin that the berth that we had been allocated had been taken and we would have to anchor, in all probability, for the whole of our projected stay. This was a great pity, for it meant that we would have to run boats to and from *Doulos* to a convenient landing-stage and, with the thousands of people expected to visit the ship and attend conferences, that could prove a real logistics problem.

Additionally, in accordance with the customs legislation, we were not permitted to open the Book Exhibition on board. This was a serious blow, as we were expecting great interest in our, by then, largely Spanish display. For a ship that was gearing up for work in Latin America the interest in Spain, we felt, would give us a good idea of the water temperature in the rest of the Spanish-speaking world.

The senior ship leaders met in conference. It was the mate who broke the news of their decision to the deck department.

'We've got to put the whole exhibition ashore, in boats.'

'Oh, is that all,' I ventured. 'I thought you were going to ask us to do something *really* difficult.'

But my irony was wasted. He was already supervising the rigging of the derricks for the task.

In fact with God, good will and hard work, the whole operation went off remarkably smoothly and, what is more, safely. All the books, tables, cabinets and associated paraphernalia were run forward on trolleys to the square of number two hatch, just in front of the bridge, made up into loads and lowered gingerly, cargo fashion, over the side into the waiting boats. Each boat alongside was firmly positioned by fore and aft lines and, although we could load only one at a time, the whole task was completed in two days, working round the clock. In fact the exhibition, set up ashore in a big marquee, was a great success and boded well for our future plans.

'Of course you mustn't forget,' said the mate helpfully, as we stood sweatily watching the last load go over the side, 'that in three weeks' time we've got to bring it all back again.' It was fortunate for him that he wasn't standing close enough to the rail for me to push him over!

But the mate's penetrating insight did have its uses. I was very interested to learn from him the following day that just across the bay was a ship-breakers' yard. I knew of such places but I had never been to one, so I was keen to accept his invitation to go ashore and take a look around.

We put on our dirtiest clothes and took the next boat. A few minutes' walk brought us to the yard and, with the mate loosely translating, we were free to look around. I followed him through the gates – and such a sight met my eyes.

The scene before us was, in the pictorial sense, the closest I had ever imagined to hell on earth. The whole vista was a collage of oily wharves and rusting hulks, heaps of jagged pipes and bars, hissing steam and flaming cutting torches. Overhead the whine of electric cranes mingled with the screech of tearing metal, as great slabs of steel – ship's side plates (there were three in the main dock being broken) were torn away from the beams and frames that had held them secure for the lifetime of the vessel, itself reduced to a ragged wreck, a skeleton without flesh in a mortuary for monarchs of the sea.

I could almost see them disintegrate before my eyes, for, no sooner had one section of plate gone, deposited on a rusty pile in a corner of the yard, than a small, voluble group of workmen would clamber up the next, flash on their torches and commence cutting. In a matter of minutes this, too, would be torn clear by the hungry crane and work would move on to the next, in a complicated but effective plan of destruction.

We picked our way carefully amongst the heaps of metal parts, pipes and almost unidentifiable objects.

'Over there! The small gear, mustn't miss that.' The mate gestured towards a pile, rudely under cover, that seemed to me no different from the others. I took his word for it.

'First we must get aboard.' He pointed towards the nearest of the three large hulks. As he spoke, there was another rending crash and an area of the foredeck of this once proud tanker disappeared into the smoke-laden sky.

'You must be joking!' I expostulated loudly, viewing the wreck with evident alarm.

'Oh, don't worry. It'll take them a good half hour to get as far as the accommodation.'

All heart, this chief officer. He led the way onto the debris-strewn deck across an oil-caked plank the width of which would have made the offering of any seventeenth-century pirate look positively generous. Thrusting aside visions of what it might be like to be suddenly hoisted aloft in a part of the accommodation surreptitiously cut from under me, I followed him boldly on board.

Immediately he began trying the lockers and cupboards, pulling open some, kicking the doors off others. I was scandalized.

'You can't do that!' I protested.

'Twenty-five minutes,' he said pointedly, adding, 'Anything we want, we pay for at the gate. You check the bridge.' He nodded towards the ladder, his hands already occupied, wresting some fire extinguisher mountings from the bulkhead.

I clambered up to the bridgewing and nervously slid open the wheel-house door. I had never done that on a strange vessel without permission before. Inside, it was a depressing sight. Gone were the familiar details that would have shown it a living ship: the clocks, barometer, radio equipment, coffee cups. All taken, or sold, as soon as she had arrived, no doubt. Hesitantly I opened one or two cupboards. It still seemed like invading someone else's privacy, another's home and work-place. There was nothing inside; a few rags and jars, perhaps. Evidently someone had made a thorough search up here already. This was going to be a fruitless exercise.

I walked the length of the spacious bridge and realized, with a shock, that I would be the last officer ever to do so.

A small painted sign caught my eye: Signal Locker. I slipped the latch, and gasped. There, in neat, ordered rows, was a complete set of flags. Galvanized into feverish activity by the find, I worked quickly along the shelves, pulling them all out onto the deck. Quickly I kicked them into a heap and, dropping a Dutch Ensign on top of them (the largest flag I could find), made them into a rough parcel, knotting the Ensign into a sack. I looked at my watch. Fifteen minutes. I must check the chart-room.

I stepped over the combing into the large many-cupboarded room at the rear of the wheel-house. Again the feel of a life lost and me the grave robber. Old, pinned notices, calendars and wall-charts hung about. But there was no equipment – all gone the way of the rest. A few old and torn charts lay on the plotting-tables and storage drawers.

Gently, out of sentiment, I slid out one flat drawer, to admire the fine old wood so soon to be destroyed for the metal on which it stood. I stared. It was full of charts!

Urgently I pulled open another, and another. They were all full. In each drawer was stacked a neatly bound canvas folio of charts. I opened one and checked the dates. Some were six months old, others nine, but certainly no more. With a few days work I could get them all up-to-date, with the corrections we carried on board *Doulos*.

I glanced about. There were seven cabinets – nearly a full world stock! Somewhere there had to be some, at least, for South America, and probably routing charts for the Atlantic.

I tore at the drawers, gradually working my way round the chartroom, and the world.

Then I had them. Three fat folios and one slim one, the latter for the Atlantic. Nearly 300 charts, just for the asking! I rolled them up tightly and staggered out into the sunlight and smoke, dragging my sack of flags. I got them, somehow, down to the main deck.

'Look,' I said stupidly, to the mate.

'No time to lose,' he urged and, swinging onto his back his own sack of swag, he made off past the grinning workmen who were already busy cutting away at the deck on which we were standing.

Like a couple of lucky cat burglars we tottered with our loads down the greasy plank onto the dockside. There was a sudden blast on a whistle and a workman gestured wildly at us. We hurried clear. The plank was kicked away and the section of deck which it had temporarily served was wrenched out of sight.

'Now you see it, now you don't,' I offered meaningfully, as we slowly retraced our steps to the gate.

'Small gear! We've forgotten the small gear!' insisted my companion. Back we went. Both my arms were heartily tired by now so, placing my burdens on a relatively clean piece of ground, I sat down on a convenient gate valve. The mate went about his business, poking around under the tattered wooden shelter. Shortly he reappeared from his temporary eclipse on the far side of the heap.

'I think you were after something like this.' He smiled and held up two azimuth rings, well used, but undamaged and of modern, prismatic design. 'They'll fit,' he said. 'Same make.' He tapped the small plate attached to each. It was the name that was on our own compass.

Silently I added them to my load, padding them carefully with flags. As we made towards the gate, I asked about price. Surely, I reasoned, these rings would fetch a good price, even second-hand. Had we enough cash?

'It's all done by weight, as if it were scrap metal, you see.'

So it was. The foreman put my flags, charts and two rings,

on the yard scale and quoted a price. The mate disagreed, so did the foreman. The mate countered, the foreman waved his hands violently and spat. I was about to point out to the mate that the foreman had more friends than we did, when they both shook hands.

'Ten pounds,' the mate said to me. 'Give or take. We'll leave the stuff here tonight. You can bring a boat round in the morning. We'd never make the landing with all this. The chief's got some engine spares to pick up as well, so you can help them out, too.'

I carefully stowed my recent finds in the corner of the foreman's hut and we struck out for the landing stage and the return boat.

Back on board, I showered, changed and went looking for Elizabeth. She was watching the sunset over the rocky outcrop that forms the natural protection for the harbour at Bilbao.

I gave her a hug and together we watched the sun touch and then embrace the rugged ground of the promontory, sinking finally out of sight, leaving only the brilliant afterglow in the sky.

'A penny for them?' she asked softly.

'God is very clever, isn't he darling.'

'Mm, you mean the sunset?'

'Something like that.'

7

Row, Men, Row!

The following day dawned bright and clear which, I suppose, is not entirely unusual in Spain, in summer. After breakfast and deck prayers, I rounded up five sailors and made my way to the boat deck and number two boat. Number two was our usual choice as errand boy, as it was small and light and easily launched.

One of the drawbacks of *Doulos* being so old was the elderly design of some of the heavy equipment, and the lifeboat davits (boat-lifting cranes) were a particular case in point. Built in the days when sailors could be hired by the boxful from the dockside, *Doulos'* davits required the muscular attention of a gang of Edwardian navvies to effect a launch. Nowadays modern davits are so light in design that a five-foot stewardess can put a boat in the water without even laddering her tights. But our lightest (number two) required at least five good men and true, and the heaviest needed more like double that number.

Brute force (some said I supplied the ignorance) was needed to swing the winding-handles which lifted the boat out over the ship's side but, once there, it was comparatively easy to lower it to the water. One vital thing to remember, however, before this happened, was the replacement of the Plug. Left out when the boat was stowed, so that rain and spray could drain away, this had to be inserted before the craft took to the water.

I once saw an impressive high-speed launch by a 'trained crew', with the boat descending smoothly and swiftly to the wave-tops, only to keep on going down as the sea rushed in through the neglected hole!

We set to winding. Strongly tempted though I was to supervise the operation from a safe distance, I conquered the inclination and took my turn at the handles, quietly puffing my thanks that this would be my only strenuous exertion for the, already warm, day. Of course, if I could have seen them, I would have noticed all the angels nearby falling about laughing at this, for I couldn't have been more wrong.

We were ready to lower. I chose two of the five to help me man the boat and sent the rest back, with thanks, to their deck work. Judging by the smiles on the faces of the former, it was an onerous task from which they had escaped for the morning. But then, they couldn't hear the angels, either.

We sat down in the boat and I gave the signal. Next stop: chief engineer. The brakeman lifted the winch brake and down we went, grinning cheerfully at a conference full of people through the panoramic windows of the lounge as we dropped past.

We drew level with the prom. deck and I held my hand up to stop, swung open the guard rail and stepped back on board once more, right outside the chief engineer's office. I knocked.

The door shot open, impelled from the inside by the impact of an engine-room boot.

'Hey arr, Cloive!' It was the chief.

Tom Moate was a man of West Country seafaring stock, with an accent that could knock the skin off a Devon rice pudding at fifty paces to prove it. For myself, I could generally catch the drift of his conversation, but some of the Chinese had big problems. However, comprehension or not, woe betide the engineer or mechanic who lost his spanner in the bilges or neglected his boiler feed pumps. Tom could convey his opinion on such matters in no uncertain terms and the miscreant felt duly chastened, whether from the inscrutable orient or otherwise.

In his younger days, Tom had served a hard apprenticeship to both man and the sea. A natural leader of men, he had combined skill and competence at his job with a style of life more reminiscent of previous centuries of seagoing. Long, roistering nights ashore in the bars and hostelries of the lesser known streets of the better known ports had led many men to regret falling under the charismatic spell of Thomas Moate.

Painting a port red, and often blue as well, was Tom's

trademark, and the more who joined him the merrier. If anyone had the dubious honour of upholding the reputation of the free-wheeling sailor, he was that man. He had lived life in the raw, rough and for real, with no holds barred. But somehow, one day, in his headlong dash, he had tripped over Jesus and, staggering to his feet, had found that, strangely and frighteningly, he had met with a true glimpse of Life. The other seemed, suddenly, no more than a wan shadow on a cloudy day. Here was Someone who possessed more quality, more depth and more distance than even he, at his breakneck pace, could cover. Being the man he was, Tom knew when he had touched the real bedrock beneath the spectacular landscape of his living – now revealed as just so many shifting sand-dunes on the face of a parched and trackless desert waste. To the astonishment and ridicule of many of his friends, Tom became a Christian.

Some time later, Tom had become involved with the first of the two ships, *Logos*, as chief engineer. Now he was bringing the very considerable weight of his experience to the second. He was a key man and a vital asset, for God had not blunted his free-wheeling and enthusiastic nature, nor his skill with machinery. Instead he filled Tom with a deep concern for the work of the ships, and a heart of gold. Many fell foul of this dominant personality during their time on *Doulos*. He suffered no fools gladly. But then, angry or perhaps hurt, they would stop and listen to the steady hiss of the air conditioning, the regular beat of the main engine, the powerful hum of the generators and know that, because God had summoned Tom, all was running well.

'G'morning, chief!'

'Arr, that it be. You'm be a takin' me ashore then, young Cloive?'

'Well, if I must. I'm not sure I want somebody's nasty, greasy, engine spares all over my nice, clean lifeboat, mind . . .'

'You'm be gettin' in the boat, me lad,' said the chief, menacingly.

I wasted no time.

We lowered to the water and, having remembered the plug,

we floated. Tom started the engine, because that is what engineers do, though I knew the procedure perfectly. I didn't want to get called a smart Alec. Too late, I feared.

The keel cut a pleasing furrow in the still, blue waters, as we sped away across the bay. The five of us (another engineer had joined his chief) looked back at the elegant white lines of the ship, as she lay peacefully at anchor. She was a fine sight.

We all waved cheerfully at a crowded motor launch that surged towards us, carrying the first of the day's visitors to the conference and discussion programmes on board. They were excited at seeing the ship, too, for they were waving, pointing and shrieking like a boat-load of school children – which, we discovered as they swept past, was exactly what they were.

We ran boats all the time in this port, never getting the use of a berth, but even so we had over 10,000 visitors to the ship. Many of them confessed later that their interest had been aroused by seeing the graceful white liner anchored out in the bay. Alongside, who knows, we might have been less accessible, certainly less visible, in amongst the other ships. Perhaps the lack of berth had worked to our advantage.

We neared the seaward entrance to the breakers' yard and the clear, blue water darkened and became opaque. A rainbow on the water here and there showed that traces of oil, like lifeblood, had crept out of the stricken beasts locked inside.

We turned the corner and I slowed the engine as we made our way between the tall slab sides of the ships we had investigated the day before. The same hissing smoke arose from their torn decks as the workmen plied their destructive trade. But down where we sat, at water level, the high rusting flanks seemed gaunt, solid features in a bleak and crumbling landscape.

'Watch out for any bits of junk in the water!' I cautioned the hand in the bow. He lifted the boat-hook in acknowledgement and then immediately began thrusting it over the side. I slowed right down. We crept in, nosing through the oily slime, towards the tiny boat quay, right under the overhanging stem of one of the hulks. Every so often the bowman raised his hand. Immediately I stopped the screw while he made scything motions at invisible horrors in the water. Then a wave, and I let in the clutch again, as softly as I dared.

'You'm be puttin' us *hard* alongside, Cloive, be'nt ee?' queried the chief with evident relish, as I looked fastidiously at the black, oil-caked wall of the dock and thought of our clean, white sides

'Crane'll not plum, else.'

'Crane, Tom? I thought you only had one or two parts to pick up?'

'Arr, right, so we do, so we do. But us might be findin' one or two of 'em sort o' fitted together, see, loike fridge compressors p'rhaps.'

'Fridge compressors?!'

He smiled. 'Don't ee worry, lad, they'll fit.' That I did not doubt, knowing his determination. But would we be stable afterwards? That, indeed was the question. In my mind I was already composing the morrow's banner headlines: 'Lifeboat Sinks Under Pile of Scrap! Crew Lost in Junk-Yard Dash!'

Elizabeth would be proud of me. 'He died in the clutch of a second-hand fridge compressor,' she would say to respectful enquirers, after my demise. 'His grave is but a pile of spare piston rings and valve collets,' she would declare with barely concealed emotion. Deeply moved they would offer her quiet but admiring sympathy.

The chief and engineer disappeared up the steps. We hung, delicately, onto the dockside. After a short interval there came a rumbling sound and the top of a mobile crane could be made out lurching its way across the yard towards us. The hook swung away and then reappeared with the first of the compressors slung beneath it. I had to admit it was a beauty – virtually brand new. The chief had certainly got a real bargain, I reflected.

It occurred to me then that while I had been dancing around the bridge of the tanker the day before, Tom and his crew had, in all probability, been wielding spanners and wrenches in the dark and cavernous interior of a derelict engine-room to secure this prize and its mate. Not a job I would envy. They had my admiration for that.

Carefully I controlled the load down onto the bench thwart amidships. I slipped the sling and the hook sailed up for number two. Experimentally, I rocked the boat. No danger so far. Down came the second, every bit as good as the first. Again I tested the boat's stability. Both weights had to be stowed high up, they were so large, and that meant a real danger of capsize. The boat lurched uncomfortably.

Regretfully I steeled myself to confront the chief. We would have to make two trips, there was nothing else for it. Then I paused. Maybe I ought to see how much more he had? Everything else would go in the bottom and would actually help the problem. I waited. It was as well I did. He appeared with an armful of things, lowering them down.

'Thur be some more up 'ere needin' 'and,' he hinted. We gave them a hand. By the time the boat was fully loaded, with his spares, plus mine and the mate's bits, it seemed as though the compressors were something of an afterthought, thrown in to make up the weight. I stepped down into the boat. Steady as a rock. Not much out of the water, mind, but steady. We all climbed in, Tom started the engine and we cast off, making a ponderous turn towards the entrance. I opened the throttle but, instead of the encouraging roar I expected, the engine gave an uncharacteristic whine, accompanied by a thumping sound on the bottom of the boat. Also, we weren't going anywhere. I closed the throttle.

'Rope round the screw,' I offered grimly to the enquiring faces turned in my direction. 'We're lower in the water, must have just caught it.' Lower in the water was an understatement, but, whatever, we were well and truly stuck now, half-way down the dock between two hulks and with no power. There was no one to hail for help, either.

One of us, and I had a shrewd idea who that might be, would have to go over the side and try to cut the rope free. With the boat so deep in the water that could prove difficult – or impossible. The very idea of diving into the murk of the dock revolted my mind. Still, it would have to be done.

The chief had different ideas. He had thought the same

thoughts and come to a different conclusion, drawn perhaps from a different era.

'Row, laddies! We've got to row!' Suiting the action to the word, he picked up the nearest oar and thrust it over the side.

'Aw, come on, Tom, it must be all of a mile!' I protested, pointing across the dock wall to the distant masts and spars – all that could be seen of our ship from the present low vantage.

'And with all this lot.' I indicated the mountain of parts on which we were perched, narrowly avoiding the term junk which had almost slipped out unbidden.

'Ah, 'tis easy. I could swim twice that before breakfast.'

I didn't doubt it, but we were the ones who would be doing the rowing, and that made all the difference in the world. Not to the chief. A gleam came to his eye, one probably well understood by his messmates of old; Tom would brook no disobedience.

'OK, OK.' I signed to the two sailors and engineer to put out the oars. We lined them up as best we could where they would not be obstructed by springs, valves, compressors and the like.

'Give way!' roared the chief, putting on his best imitation of a Roman galley master. He wouldn't have needed much training if he'd been offered the job, that was clear. We dipped our oars.

'And again! In . . . out! In . . . out!' He called the time and we responded. So, eventually, did the lifeboat and we made painful and crablike progress out of the dock. A few fishermen paused to watch us from the end of the jetty as we pulled around, like a top-heavy water beetle in slow motion, before setting out across the bay. They gave no sign of recognition, or even of very much interest. One spat roundly onto the stone of the quay, possibly expressing some sympathy with our predicament. A powerful thing, the fellowship of the sea. I was minded to shout for a bit of assistance but had the strongest feeling that the fellowship might need the reassurance of something that jangled in the pocket, and we had nothing, having paid for our cargo the day before. I held my peace and grunted vengefully at the oar.

'In . . .out! In . . . out!' Slowly, so slowly, we left the jetty behind. I entertained another hope: the visitors' launch might see us and come to our aid. We were clearly visible now, surely one would soon be passing? The hope soon died. It was lunchtime and after that, the siesta. The boats had stopped running for the time being. I gave it another moment of life: the watch officer on deck (we all kept twenty-four hour anchor watches) would see us and send help.

Nothing came. Hope expired. I learned later that he had seen us but felt we were doing so well that we needed no assistance. I soon put him right on that score. We remain friends.

'*IN . . . OUT! IN . . . OUT!*' The sun grew hotter, the chief louder and our hands redder. Our backs ached under the crack of the lash, our parched tongues lolled out, gasping for water . . . well, perhaps I exaggerate, but we certainly steamed gently, I'm sure of that.

Eventually, we ran alongside. Just in time to catch the after-lunch rail leaners, who provided an appreciative audience as we splashed up to the davit falls to hook on.

'*OARS!*' Shouted the chief, calling us to stop. There was a round of applause from above, possibly he even bowed. Captain Hook returning with the treasure.

Once lightened and hoisted up to the prom. deck, willing hands soon removed our vital cargo, to be rapidly swallowed up in the engine-room. The two compressors were soon set to work and later, when running, actually did the work of no less than twelve smaller ones, which had been in various states of irrecoverable decay.

Back on the boat-deck, some sympathetic sailors appeared to help us with the wind in. We couldn't have managed it ourselves.

The mate came by just as I was checking the final lashings.

'Good to help out the engineers now and then, isn't it Clive? Work together and all that, team spirit, eh? Great stuff!'

He paused to lift his purchases out of the boat and looked for a moment at the greasy water-line mark around the middle of the hull and the black marks on the fenders.

'Oh, you will make sure that this is all nice and clean again when you've finished, won't you? Can't have the lifeboats looking like oiling barges, can we?'

God is good to me on occasions like these. He has given me an even temper.

8
Superdad

'Darling, I really don't feel very well.'

Elizabeth was sitting, looking rather pale, on the day-bed in our cabin, with little baby Richard, now just seven months, balancing unsteadily on her knee. He gurgled excitedly at the sight of his father.

'I'm sorry love, but I really haven't time to stop now. You know we're sailing tomorrow morning. Try a couple of aspirins.'

I am renowned for the deep sympathy which I offer to sick people, especially those close to me. But it was true that I was very busy. We all were, with sailing day close upon us. The books had to be loaded, compass set up, courses checked. A hundred and one things were claiming my attention. It was most inconsiderate of Elizabeth to be feeling ill before sailing day. No doubt she'd pull through. Powerful things, aspirins.

I returned to the cabin an hour later to find the doctor in attendance.

'Clive, your wife has a temperature of 105. I've ordered her straight to bed. She'll stay there for two or three days at least. She's sleeping now, don't disturb her, will you?'

I was all concern and contrition.

'Oh, ah, I mean no. She'll be all right, won't she?'

'When the fever comes down. But she needs rest and sleep.'

He paused and cocked an ear.

'Meanwhile, it sounds as though you have some duties to attend to.'

'Well, of course I . . .' I stopped. The doctor was not referring to my pressing work on deck. A low-key wail had just started next door and was penetrating the thin partition that separated us from Richard.

'Ah, yes.'

'You'll call me when she wakes, won't you?' He picked up his bag. 'Bye!'

The doctor left, with a ghost of a smile flickering around the corners of his bedside manner.

The wailing was getting louder.

I peeped around the curtain that divided our bed from the rest of the cabin. Elizabeth, drawn-faced, lay helplessly on the pillow. Her eyes were closed, her breathing regular but shallow. I felt ashamed of my earlier indifference. Lightly I kissed her burning forehead. She made no response.

'Sorry love,' I murmured. 'Didn't realize you see, very busy . . .'

This sentimental and one-sided reconciliation was increasingly drowned by the animated barrage of complaint emanating from behind the partition. At this, Elizabeth did stir, the cries making their point even through drugged and fevered sleep. It was time to act. I braced myself to my duty.

A verse or two of the Immortal Bard sprang to mind, as I made for the door: 'Once more unto the breeches, dear friends, once more . . .' I plucked the protesting junior member of the family from the damp recesses of his travelling-cot and set to work.

My watch said noon, a good thirty minutes to lunch. Time enough to change and feed him, I thought.

I never made it to lunch. Not that I was entirely inept at the task of baby-handling, I hasten to add. I had served a brief apprenticeship at the hands of Elizabeth but, somehow, without the experienced directions of the expert, which had always hitherto been available, everything seemed to take a great deal longer. Changing the nappy *alone* took the whole of the planned half-hour – and that hadn't been the complaint, which I had correctly interpreted as a demand for food. Still, he enjoyed the new game with Daddy unexpectedly in charge and joined in playfully to make it last as long as possible – kicking everything off at the last moment, when I had it held together and was about to secure the pin.

The thought of food then returned to him. It was fortunate that Elizabeth had stopped feeding him herself (on joining ship, at the start), or I might have been up against more than I could handle. At least all I had to do was find the powdered stuff he was currently enjoying and mix up a batch. No problem, provided you knew the quantities and where the bottles were, where the teats were, and that they had been sterilized (Elizabeth had always stressed the importance of sterilizing the teats), and could put your hand on the right container of ready-cooled boiled water. Simple really.

I searched the cabin. I searched the pantry. Milk powder I found, including instructions. Boiled water I found. Measures and bottle I found. But sterilized teats – no way.

Richard had reached the final stages of terminal starvation, and possibly vocal expression, as he was almost hoarse, by the time I had located the bowl, carefully secured against the possible motion of the ship and therefore hidden from view, containing the required items. Urgently I prepared the mixture, which proved very sticky when spilt (as it frequently was), and plugged Richard in. He seemed somehow more endearing with the bottle filling that raucous little mouth. At least the cries were silenced.

I began, unreasonably perhaps, to feel pleased with myself. I had met the challenge and triumphed. After all, who needed lunch?

About three-quarters of the way down, interest flagged. I unplugged. Now for the winding; at least I knew what to do there. Up on the shoulder and a gentle rub on the back. I was rewarded with a gentle burp and a slight cough. There was a warm feeling, suddenly, around my shoulder blade. I lifted Richard off and felt the patch with my hand. It came away warm and sticky.

'Oh, Richard,' I sighed, and reached for a cloth. Richard looked at me and smiled. There was a cloud of doubt in his eyes but it soon cleared to the accompaniment of a low rumbling in his tummy area. He smiled again. A faint aroma drifted across the cabin.

Oh, Richard!' I cried. 'You haven't?' Inspection proved, unfortunately, that he had. I bent to the drawer for a fresh nappy. It was going to be a long afternoon.

The day wore on. Finally fed and watered, and mainly dry, Richard now needed amusing. Here we reached something of a compromise. He came up to the chart-room and helped with the courses. This was great fun and he enjoyed himself tremendously, until he felt he should add his own corrections to my carefully inscribed handiwork by launching the chart pencils on brief trajectories across the table.

We moved on to the gyro compass, which needed some adjustment. This also was a hit, its flashing lights and whirling noises evidently much superior to the rattles and squeaking ducks of an average afternoon.

Work, however, had to be broken down into sections to allow for early afternoon snack and change, mid-afternoon tea and change, late tea and change, etc., etc. All said and done, I was somewhat behind on the day when Elizabeth woke at five and I called the doctor, in accordance with instructions.

'Good,' commented the doctor, on taking her pulse and temperature. 'Another two or three days in there and you'll be well on the way to recovery.'

'Oh, great,' I enthused in reply, patting Elizabeth warmly on the arm as she smiled weakly up at me.

'You'll soon be on the mend. Richard will be pleased too, he's missed you a lot . . .' The full horror of the discussion suddenly became apparent. I swung round on the doctor.

'Two or three days!' I gasped. 'I can't possibly cope for two or three days!'

There I was, starving hungry, mountains of evil-smelling nappies to wash, piles of sticky bottles to cure, the navigational preparations of the ship in chaos – and Elizabeth had only been out of action for one afternoon! What it would be like after two or three days beggared the imagination.

'I'll see the girls' leader,' promised the doctor. 'She may be able to find someone to help out in the evenings.'

'I'll need a whole lot more than the evenings, if you want this ship to get to Lisbon,' I answered grimly, mentioning our next and eagerly anticipated port of call. The doctor saw that I was a desperate man.

'OK, OK, maybe we can arrange a roster, or something. I'm sure that Nurse Gretchen can help you out tonight. I won't be needing her in the surgery.'

I wasn't sure I believed the latter part of his statement, but delivered, as it had been, in a sort of 'your need is greater than mine' tone of voice, I was in full agreement with the conclusion.

Nurse Gretchen was wonderful. She came over and introduced herself to us at supper, something I had determined not to miss, whatever the state of Richard's stomach or functions. Thankfully I handed over to her the responsibility of bedtime while I went out on deck to attend, belatedly, to the various arrangements for the morrow's sailing.

One thing that had lain heavily on all our minds had been the problem of obtaining a berth in Lisbon. We had been offered a number of old cargo berths, distant from the city centre and only for a few days. It seemed as though we would have to anchor, or to move berth regularly – highly unsatisfactory for the particular work of the ship. I dropped by the programme office to see if there was any change. There wasn't. The team that had gone ahead to Lisbon had made no progress. There was a prayer meeting starting now, would I be going? I declined, for more needed doing and, anyway, I had to drop in to see how Gretchen was coping. I realized with a guilty start that I had just left her to get on with it.

I hurried back to the cabin. But I needn't have worried. Gretchen was a model of calm efficiency and a tangible aura of competent authority surrounded her every move. The nappies seemed to jump properly into place at her very presence, the pins slid snugly home, the bottle feed mixed up promptly at the first attempt, with no sticky surplus. Even Richard knew he was in the hands of a professional and uttered nary a squeak or a moan. This might not be as much fun as Daddy, but boy, it was on time and in place, no messing. Speedily he was washed and readied for bed, while I darted out and completed a memo or two on the bridge, before coming down to give him his goodnight kiss.

Gretchen was already singing him to sleep, and a drowsy

gurgle floating out of the open port-hole as I passed told me that her ministrations were having the desired effect. He scarcely noticed my presence, as she continued rocking him in her arms preparatory to laying him gently in his cot. I looked at them both in the shaded nursery light. The stranger mothering my child, her poise and features a picture of total concern. Richard slipping peacefully to sleep in her arms. With a shock of sudden delight, I realized that she was singing to him in German. Her own language of the nursery.

It was, I suppose, a small thing to touch me so much, but in a way it seemed to me to represent the largeness of our purpose on board. In the deepest sense, the ship was home to neither of us — and our backgrounds were so visibly different. Yet we had made it a community and a home, to reach out to others. Gretchen had created a nursery here for my child, in her own way, but to serve my need. Tomorrow I would be serving hers by guiding the ship onward with my skills.

I was seeing, it seemed to me at that moment, the essence of Love Himself abiding and at work in that room. I closed the door softly and stepped into our cabin to sit quietly for a few minutes with Elizabeth, who was herself asleep.

Her fever abated very little that night and, as I had expected, I spent the night on the day-bed. Our bed, a single man's bunk in the ship's old cruising days, was too narrow for comfort at the best of times. Now she needed all the comfort she could get.

It was a wakeful night. Richard woke twice and Elizabeth once, for something to drink. Her fever had given her a raging thirst and, although I had had the doctor's reassurance, I spent some time lying uncomfortably on the makeshift cushions praying simply to God for her renewed strength and health.

It was the sort of prayer that goes up, by the million, every day and every hour of the day around the world — the prayer for an abatement of suffering for a loved one. My prayers had, perhaps, a tinge of further disquiet in that my wife was certainly suffering as a direct result of our commitment to serve our fellow men in God's name. The virus, for that is what it was, had obviously been contracted locally, possibly through contact with one of our thousands of visitors.

Here, as in any port, anyone who wished could come on board, provided they had the patience to queue. Jesus had turned no one away and neither could we, if we were to represent his concern for the countries we visited. But it seemed unfair that the problems we, as a family, had already foreseen and faced should be increased by this unpleasant illness. God had not prevented it.

I have found myself in similar situations, asking similar questions, a number of times since then and I have never received a written reply. But I suppose, in an odd way, out of it came a deeper love for Elizabeth and also a healthy respect for her ability quietly to cope with the very basic problems of bringing up a family. If I had ever been tempted before, I could never again envy Elizabeth her daily round. Maybe there was a holy lesson in there somewhere.

In any case, when the deck lights that reflected on the port-hole curtains grew dim in the brighter glow of the stretching fingers of dawn I was still awake. I knew I had had little sleep and felt as if I'd had none. Rising, I dressed myself and then Richard, who was already stirring, and we slipped out quietly for an early morning walk before breakfast.

The open decks were deserted and we wandered down to see the gangway watchman just to break the loneliness of the morning by talking to someone. It was Roberto, who had been with us from Genoa, the only Italian on board. As usual his head was deep in a book, for he loved to read. But his book was in English, for he also badly wanted to learn the language. He looked up.

'Gooda morning,' he said slowly, smiling and tickling Richard under the chin. 'You hava heard, eh?'

'No, what?' I replied, wondering what information could be so interesting as to open a conversation at this hour.

'We have a berth in Lisbon! The very best, used for all the ships with people, you know the big ones . . .' His English failed him.

'We've got the passenger ship berth?'

'Ah, yes, si. Is good, no?'

It seemed that God had been at work that night, after all.

9

Mooring-Party, Stand By!

The River Tagus glinted brightly in the morning sunlight as we made our slow turn around the headland into the estuary. Lisbon, the capital city of Portugal, lies on the northern bank, but inland from the river mouth; at present we could see only the steep cliffs on the north shore on our port bow. To starboard there seemed still to be open sea, but in reality the unbroken blue water hid a deceptive ridge of shoals and sandbanks, sediment deposited by the river in its continual meeting with the Atlantic Ocean.

Ahead, the pilot launch, hurrying out to meet us, was buffeting sturdily against the short onshore chop stirred up by the steady ocean breeze. Its little recognition pennant, code flag H, flapped and dipped in the slipstream and spray. It was a splendid day, for the wind had taken the heat out of the sun, but it was warm enough to bask in.

Elizabeth was sitting beside me, in the nearest thing to a deck chair that *Doulos* possessed, with Richard, in his chequered sunhat, playing energetically on a rug beside her. I was fielding the toys. It was her first day out of doors since her illness, from which she was now recovering, though still weak from the fever. I was hoping the sun and sights would lift her rather dampened spirits, and my potion appeared to be working.

Because of the late arrival (we usually aimed to make a port in the early morning) I was off watch and could enjoy the show with her, as the river scenery and, later, the historic city unfolded to our view. I would be working later, of course, when it came to mooring, but for the moment I could enjoy the day. I poured out another glass of the fresh orange juice, pressed from stock bought in Spain, and we watched the approaching boat make its wide U-turn to run in alongside and discharge its official passenger: our pilot for the river passage. *Doulos* slowed for his convenience and safety as he leaped from boat to boarding-ladder and climbed his way up our sheer white flanks to disappear through the entry port, to join the captain on the bridge.

We were soon under way again and shortly we could make out, low down on the shore where the river began to narrow, the medieval castle known as Belem, after the Portuguese colony established on the lower reaches of the Amazon in the seventeenth century. We were not to know it then, as we admired the waving flags and quaintly sculptured stone battlements of the keep but, almost two years later, we were to look down from these same decks on the castellations of its namesake when *Doulos* ventured up-river to stay in the heartland of the lower Amazon basin.

Quaint and toy-like it may have looked at a distance, but close to, and under the guns, Belem looked a lot less playful. The river constrained all ships to close the shore at this point and I discovered later, on my visit to the local maritime museum, that the castle had proved a keystone in the seaward defence of the city for centuries.

We swung gently to starboard and the vista of the city opened up before us. Directly ahead, through the ropes, wires and derricks which surrounded the mast, we could see the great red-arched bridge that spans the river at its lowest crossing-point, and under which we would be berthing at the passenger terminal. Over to our right, at the south end of the span, rose the massive statue of Christ the King, his arms outstretched towards the city. When we visited Rio de Janiero, many months later, we saw his copy, also welcoming us in. For Brazil still retains its many ties with Portugal, reminders of its colonial history.

At the other end, the bridge pointed to the city itself. Possibly one of the most colourful ports in the world, Lisbon stretched down towards us from the bridge-head and away far into the distance, where the higher buildings began, and the quays and dockyards cut the riverbank. It also rose up the hillside to red-roofed houses, green trees and partial hanging gardens with, here and there a gleam of white marble from some elderly edifice, and the yellow of the higher, unmetalled streets and poorer homes.

There was flesh on the bones of this city and the pulse of life flowed in its streets. It felt a community as well as a centre for commerce and trade. Trolley buses and trams clanged along the riverside roads. Traffic roared and hooted on the highways, and busy boats, tugs, pleasure craft and fishing smacks crossed and recrossed the water ahead.

Elizabeth was enchanted. I, who had seen so many ports of the world before, including Lisbon, now saw it with her eyes and had to admit to a similar excitement, though it was pretty well concealed.

Very soon we passed the statue and monument to King Henry the Navigator, and I evidenced open interest. King Henry was the first man in the western world to develop a comprehensive and logical system of ocean navigation. He looked at the stars, plotted their courses and wrote down his results. This became the first Nautical Almanac, an indispensable tool still in full use in its modern form on ships today. He travelled far to prove his theories and made many of the first conquests of the Portuguese Empire. With navigation established, sea power had come to stay. I gave his imaginative memorial, a ship's prow set about with leaping monsters and plotting instruments, a respectful nod of appreciation as we passed.

We were approaching the bridge and the berth. The public address system crackled to life. Through the roar of the traffic thundering overhead I made out the pipe:

'Harbour stations, harbour stations, mooring parties stand by fore and aft.'

I squeezed Elizabeth's hand and leapt energetically up the bridge ladder to collect my walkie-talkie, finding the mate at the top.

'Five and two, I think, will do us,' he commented, offering me my radio. He was telling me the number and position of the ropes he wanted out.

'Good long leads, too. There's quite a current.'

Very wise, as we were berthing in the main river, where the weight of water would be pulling us downstream all the time. Down aft, my mooring party stood waiting. They looked assured and confident, more like sailors now. Quite different from the nervous bunch of students I had met in Genoa. There I had had to talk every movement through before attempting it, kicking each rope to identify it, and leading them, literally, by the hand to their stations.

Now, I noticed, they had prepared the heaving lines – the light, weighted ropes thrown ashore first on which the others would be sent. They had uncovered the bins and fairleads, the forearm-sized mooring-lines lay already 'flaked out' in compact rows on the deck, ready to run. They were learning. Although by no means able seamen yet, they had certainly passed the 'ready and willing' stage and were, maybe, getting to be just a little more than ordinary.

I quickly ordered the capstan tested and two heaving-lines bent on the thick rope loops, or 'bights', of the heavy mooring-lines. I still had to be very careful when mooring up for, although my deckmen knew something of the job, they still knew very little of what could go wrong, or even the danger signs. With 7,000-odd tons of ship waving around on the end of our ropes, it didn't need much to go awry for a nasty accident to strike. I had to jangle the alarm bells for all of them and couldn't afford a moment of inattention. I had found that the key to the operation was simply to take each stage more slowly than I would have done with trained seamen, no matter what heat was on. This often infuriated the captain and pilot on the bridge, but they were a world away and I could always turn the volume on the radio down if matters became too charged.

The pilot's reputation could afford a few dents. So, come to that, could the doughty old hull of the great lady herself. But my sailors could not, and that was the way it was going to stay.

A berthing-tug nosed fussily up to the stern quarter and a heaving-line whistled out from her fo'c'sle to a shout of warning. The weighted end bounced on the deck and hit the steering house with a smack. A deckman caught it, and several others tailed on to heave a heavy wire up through the protective fairlead and over the upright bitts, which could take the whole weight of the vessel, if needed.

I was pleased: tug's line. That meant that we had one more of our own to play with. In the complicated and confined spaghetti-house that the aft mooring position would soon become, one extra could come in handy. Although seven or eight ropes would soon be lying over each other, leading over the side in different directions – some taking the strain, others hanging loose, some needing securing and others letting go – I had to keep them all in mind. Add to that knowledge of the position of the ship, her intentions, work of tugs, nearness of quay, the possible dangers to inexperienced sailors and you can see how time flies when you are enjoying yourself.

More seriously, I found the invariable good humour of the crew, and their willingness to help each other out, of real assistance. They didn't answer back, or complain, or needle me. They were, in fact, close friends, making the job much safer than it may have appeared. To my recollection there has not been one mooring accident to date on board, and that with several changes of crew and officers.

'Send away the stern line!' rattled the radio.

'Aye, aye!' I motioned to the well-muscled sailor by my side, an art student in Paris six months before. He held the coiled heaving-line in his hands. Carefully he lifted half of the turns and drew back his throwing-hand. He swung it up and over. The line rushed out and the coils whipped free of his grasp as it flew towards the quay. But he had misjudged the wind and the line fell, shamefully, a few yards short of the waiting hands ashore. There was a gleeful groan from the off-duty staff lining the deck above. He looked rueful and glanced at me.

'Get it in, get it in,' I muttered fussily. It should have been pulled in the moment the wind had caught it. It was obvious to me that it couldn't have made it. I stopped myself. He was doing his best. In different circumstances I doubt if I could have recognized a Renoir, or a Monet – something he could probably do in his sleep. I was lucky to get the line thrown decently at all.

'When you're ready,' I added more gently. He made it with the second throw and was rewarded by a cheer from the spectators. The two men at the fairlead quickly fed the large mooring-rope out over the side in response to my frantic hand-flapping. It looked like a monstrous black-and-white python, with the bight for a head, as it hissed through the water, pulled quickly by the light line and the mooring-gang ashore.

They laid hold of the big eye and manhandled it up onto the quay, dropping it over the nearest bollard. With shouts and waves they indicated I could now heave it in. I was not so sure. Reluctant as I might have been to overtax their limited strength, the place where they had left my rope was not where I wanted it to stay. Long leads the mate had said and long leads it was going to be.

'No, no, NO!' I shouted in my best gale-force voice, waving my radio in circles in the air.

'Next one down – that way – THERE!' I pointed with both arms to the next bollard along and then to the rope. I must have resembled a sea scout at semaphore on a windy day. Despite this entertaining performance my target audience suddenly seemed devoid of hearing. They looked at one another with sudden and unusual interest, discussed, possibly, the splendid weather, and generally gazed anywhere but at the ship.

What, I asked myself, would Henry the Navigator have done under the circumstances? Fortunately help came from a different quarter: a compatriot. A Portuguese crew member called down from the deck above, where he had been enjoying the proceedings.

'What's the problem?'

I explained as briefly as I could.

He nodded and then unleashed a tirrade of instructions onto the group below. They turned around at the shock of hearing their own language from a foreign ship. Then, having admitted their ability to hear, they reluctantly picked up the rope and marched it off to the waiting bollard.

'Heave away!' I yelled, when it was in place. The man on the capstan control glued his eyes to the position of my hand as I, in turn, watched the rope and signalled it taut.

'Coming up!' I cautioned, as it came clear of the water and, waving him to slow down, I brought it to light tension. Any snatching would be very dangerous and could easily melt the man-made fibre of the rope. I thumbed the radio.

'Line ashore aft, heaving away.'

'Well done aft, what kept you?' The condescension in the voice was only marginally distorted.

'Ah, yes, well we weren't sure if the natives were friendly, at first.'

'Send away your spring, aft,' was all the reply I apparently deserved. We sent out our second line, in the opposite direction to the first. In this position it had a dampening and elastic effect on the ship's movement along the quay – hence its name. As the tug pushed, we slid slowly into position, heaving steadily on both ropes.

'In position. Make fast!' The 'stopper' men bent to their task and wrapped a double length of small rope around the taut bar of the heavy mooring-line. They stood back, holding both ends.

'Come back!'

The capstan driver put his lever to reverse and the whole weight came on the double strands of light rope. Quickly the turns on the drum were cast off by urgent hands and entwined, figure of eight fashion, around the waiting bitts. This done, the stopper ropes were carefully slipped off and eased clear. The bitts now took the weight through the mooring-rope and the capstan was free for another. The spaghetti was piling up, but the work was going smoothly.

At last I straightened from my position by the forward bitts.

'All fast aft, at five and two,' I relayed to the bridge. 'Er, may we let the tug go now?' I added innocently, for it had apparently been forgotten and, unusually quiescent for one of its kind, had not made the fact known.

'Good grief, hasn't it gone yet?!'

'Well, it could be a whale with a green funnel, I suppose.'

'Let go the tug aft,' came the pained and formal request.

'Aye, aye.'

A pause, a splash and the heavy beating of a diesel as our

assistant pulled clear under full power, giving us a brief toot on her whistle.

'Tug gone and clear aft.'

'Aye, aye. Pipe down aft.'

I looked around at the ordered disarray of secured ropes and the men who had been responsible, leaning back tired and half-amazed at their own achievement.

'Thank you, gentlemen,' I said, meaning it.

10
A Cup of Black Coffee

Our stay in Lisbon ended with an unexpected request from the port authorities to vacate our much-appreciated berth and go to anchor for the final three days of our visit. This would have proved no real problem, for the bulk of our work was completed, except for the fact that a team of six or so had taken a van inland. Telephone messages to Post Offices on their intended route failed to find them, and we reluctantly concluded that we would have to abandon them to the shock of returning and finding us gone. The ship's local agent would meet them, we hoped.

In fact the situation was saved by the sensible action of the junior second officer, one of the team, who, realizing what had happened, drove along the riverside until he espied our riding-lights in the anchorage. He then swung the van towards us and commenced a long conversation with me on the bridge by means of the headlights, flashing in morse code. The gist of the message being: Why had they been stranded? Was it something that they'd said? And what were we intending to do about it?

I replied on the ship's signal lamp to the effect that these matters were all out of our hands. We were prevented from sending boats at night for customs reasons and trusted that they would find the night a short one, the dawn bringing new hope and succour, etc.

However, as indicated, the man was not without resource and, having blinked us a generous goodnight, he drove off to the home of some local friends, who were delighted at having such a large party to entertain, fed them fully and bedded them down in luxurious comfort. A Latin phrase comes to mind for the justice of this conclusion.

I often wonder what the Portuguese authorities made of our suspicious flashing across the harbour during the evening, but we heard nothing more. The government changed quite soon after we left, however, so maybe they thought that the revolution was at hand, and decided to go quietly. One never knows.

From Portugal we sailed on south, through the straits of Gibraltar. They were shrouded in mist at the time, which was a pity for the sightseers. It was also a pity for me, as the radar decided to take a break and blanked out on me. This left us blind for fifteen minutes while the radio officer attempted to revive it.

'All it needs is a little patience,' he explained. 'It's no good just booting it.'

I concurred readily, concealing the fact that I had already tried that remedy. He knew.

'They don't like it you know, *especially* these nine-centimetre jobs; very sensitive, nine-centimetres are.'

I drifted off and concerned myself with the minor problem of what we were likely to hit first – Africa or Europe. In the event we did neither, for I did what you should never do at such moments and followed the ship ahead. He didn't look too lost and his radar was going round. It was a reasonable answer.

Eventually the radio officer stood up, glanced surreptitiously over his shoulder, and gave the cabinet a good thump with his fist. It sprang to life.

'Oh, well done,' I enthused. 'Jolly impressive. I'll try to remember next time. Lots of patience, huh?'

He smiled through his teeth: 'No problem, no problem, always pleased to advise, any time.'

We arrived at the holiday port of Malaga and, after a prolonged stay left for the UK, well satisfied with the progress made. Malaga had proved a fitting climax to our shake-down voyage. Over 50,000 visitors on board and great interest and involvement shown.

We returned to London, with a quick refuelling stop in Flushing, and the ship was honoured by a visit from the then Archbishop of Canterbury, Donald Coggan. He was not the first, and certainly not the last, of the many distinguished men and women whom I was to meet, and receive, on board.

London was a busy time for us all. There were some major

conferences to be arranged, refurbishing work to be done and final preparations to be made for the Atlantic crossing to North and then, finally, South America. But we were well satisfied with the ship and her operation. There had been, quite naturally, a number of teething troubles, though these should more properly have been called ageing troubles.

The new systems – such as the book exhibition, lifts, rack stowage, print shop and others had run well and the fresh crew had matured to seasoned hands. But if our crew was practised and ready, and the ship broken in to her new life, a cloud was beginning to hang over our own involvement in the project.

Richard had become ill.

We weren't worried at first. An upset tummy is not entirely unusual for a British constitution eating, or drinking, in foreign parts. But it wouldn't stop. He could keep nothing down and his weight began to drop. We became more concerned. The weeks went by and, although he seemed a normal healthy boy, his stomach wouldn't fall into line. The medical staff made many suggestions, as did almost everyone else. We hopefully tried them all, but with such a small child many of the more powerful remedies for such a condition were prohibited for fear of deadly side-effects. There was no improvement.

In London, we went to see a doctor ashore. She gave it to us straight. The ship was no place for baby Richard in that condition. We had to agree. I went to see the ship director. He understood at once, but looked baffled:

'It's very strange,' he commented, 'but every other deck officer will be changing too.' I was surprised.

'We were kind of counting on you to give us some continuity and experience. Even the captain will be new.'

I apologized, but again explained my reasons. He agreed to sign me off. Elizabeth and Richard left the ship and I arranged to follow as soon as I could tie things up.

But, pray as we might, no new second officer appeared to take my place. Sailing day drew near. The new captain called me to his cabin. The ship director and chief officer were there as well.

'Clive, is there any hope of you staying on just for the Atlantic passage? We could fly you home from the States on arrival.'

I was torn. I could see that my experience would be valuable on a trans-ocean passage – the first, as far as we were concerned. I also wanted, naturally, to be with Elizabeth, who had been summarily dumped, with a sick baby, onto some hospitable friends. However, I was being asked for weeks only, not months, and it was pretty vital that *Doulos* made the passage safely.

I consented to go. Sighs of relief from the assembled company. I offered my excuses and slipped up to the chart-room, pulling open the drawers and sharpening the pencils. I had some homework to do. We were sailing within forty-eight hours.

The route I eventually agreed with the captain was down to the Azores and then across. Our destination was Portsmouth, Virginia. The leg south to the Azores would, we hoped, ensure avoiding bad weather in the North Atlantic and also give us a better landfall on the US coast.

Unusually, we sailed on time and, as we dipped our way south-west past Lands End, I went up on the bridge for the last lighthouse – Bishop Rock. I was officially not on watch until later, but the 'departure fix' is important – all the calculations for the voyage, until land is again sighted, depend upon it – so I wanted to make sure myself.

I took a good, long look through the azimuth mirror at the winking beacon, said a murmured goodbye to Elizabeth, and went inside to check the radar range. I drew the lines in carefully on the chart and noted the fix neatly in the deck Log and my own notebook. These figures would provide the basis for my 'noon' calculations the next morning when, out of sight of land, we would be relying on the smiling sun to tell us where we had got to. With a little help from my sextant, of course.

It was an interesting problem. Steaming out into the Atlantic, I had to find a tiny dot in the middle: St Michael, one of the larger Azores. In four days' time we would either find it or miss it. Romantic? No, more a matter of a few pages of closely-worked calculations. Of course it was romantic!

With the steady decrease of latitude came an increase in temperature, and everyone on board was relieved to give up wearing the heavy sweaters and coats they had donned to ward off the autumn chills of England. We weren't going far enough south to be really tropical, but it was pleasant to be warm again.

We sped on south-west. My sights seemed to agree with those of the first officer, who gazed at the stars in the morning and evening, while I gazed at the sun mid-day. It was towards me as navigator, however, that the captain directed his interest on the evening of the fourth day.

'Well, Vasco, when's it to be?' He wanted my estimate of our time to landfall on St Michael. The lighthouse of the same name on the north-east tip of the island would be our first sighting, if I had got my sums right.

A familiar panic gripped me at the question. I had made a hundred landfalls, some good, some not so good, some on time, others unexpectedly late or early, due to the motions of unknown currents and tides. Every day I confidently signed the 'noon chit', a small slip of paper giving the captain the daily position and distance run. My figures looked fine, the distillation of several hours work, mine and the first officer's.

But supposing an unseen error had crept in? Prepackaged into the regular columns of figures, this would grow, little by little – a mathematical cancer – until the tidy sums represented a tissue of lies, with no basis in fact at all. Neat but nonsense. Perhaps we would miss St Michael altogether and steam for ever south-westward, eternally searching for the lost island . . . My imagination was beginning to take hold. I glanced at my note-book.

'03.00, sir!' Taking all things into account, that was my educated guess. It could just have easily been '01.00, sir!', or '04.00, sir!' But I had made my bid. Three a.m. tomorrow it was.

'Well, we'll see,' smiled the captain. 'Thank you.' A picture of doubtful courtesy, born of very many years' experience of young navigators, and the temperament of a gentleman.

'Your watch, then,' he commented. 'Call me when you get

something.' He had confidence in me. He had said 'when' and not 'if'.

The telephone by my bunkside clamoured for attention. I peered sleepily at luminous hands. Quarter to midnight. Fighting sleep, I unhitched the instrument. The breezy tones of the third officer greeted me.

'Fifteen minutes to your watch,' he noted cheerfully. He could afford to; he would soon be in bed.

Thirteen minutes later, I was greeting him face to face.

'What's cooking?' I enquired hopefully.

'Your coffee's about all.' He pointed to the chart and the steady line of pencil crosses indicating where we thought we were, according to my calculated approach. He had faithfully maintained the estimate. He gestured forward into the blackness of the night.

'Nothing so far.' He handed over the watch: course, speed, errors, etc.

'Got the weight?'

I sipped at my cup of strong black coffee, before replying.

'Yep, no problem. Shouldn't be able to see anything yet anyway,' I added.

'Well, quite.' He left the bridge.

The minutes ticked by. My brain revived slowly with the help of the coffee. The helmsman changed. An hour gone.

'Wheel relieved by Johansen, sir, two three eight.'

'Steering two three eight, aye, aye.'

'Look-out relieved by Chico, sir, nothing in sight.'

'Nothing in sight, aye, aye.'

Two o'clock came and went. I toyed ineffectually with the radio direction finder. A very helpful thing around the European coast, the lack of long-range stations made it wildly inaccurate in mid-Atlantic. I switched it off in disgust. Three a.m.

'Hey, Chico.'

'Serr?'

'How about some more coffee, eh?'

'OK, Serr.'

There was a sudden commotion outside. The look-out's face

appeared suddenly through the curtain.

'There's a buoy out there!'

I grabbed the binoculars and followed him outside. Low, fine on the starboard bow, was a small, dim light. I knew it couldn't be a buoy – too deep, though it certainly looked like one. It flashed. I counted the pulses. St Michael's Point light! It must have been operating on much-reduced power, which was why we hadn't seen the loom of it before. I took a bearing and noted the time: two minutes past three. Not bad, eh? I glowed for a minute or two in the corner of the chart-room as I laid off the fix. Then I telephoned the captain.

'Oh, *good* morning, sir, second officer here! St Michael's light sighted at 03.02, sir!'

'Well, that was when you expected it, wasn't it?'

I could only agree.

We stopped in the Azores, stepping-stones of the Atlantic, for only two days. We had to press on for America. En route lay yet more trials for my magnetic personality. The captain felt that the magnetic, 'back-up' compass, which was sited above the bridge on a deck known as the 'monkey island', would offer little back-up in the event of a gyro compass failure. It needed a thorough clean, he said. Since it was part of the navigation equipment, guess who got the job? I unshipped the bowl and dismantled it in the corner of the wheel-house. It was a liquid compass, which contains a good few pints of pure alcohol to damp its movement. Alcohol is used so that it will not freeze in winter. I poured all of this into a large jug and stowed it in the spare-gear cupboard, along with the other parts of the deranged compass. It would keep until the morrow. All work and no play, etc.

That night, as we rolled across the dark and seamless waste of the North Atlantic, I asked Johansen for my usual cup of black stuff. He was happy to oblige, and busily got cracking with the bridge kettle. I wandered out to talk to the look-out, in the confident hope that a smiling Johansen would shortly appear bearing two steaming mugs of coffee.

What emerged from the wheel-house door a matter of minutes later was neither Johansen nor coffee, but the overpowering aroma of strong spirit. Though tempted to jump to the conclusion that Johansen and the helmsman had instantly embarked on a wild, drunken party I felt that, considering the circumstances, this was unlikely. It was with a markedly puzzled expression that I leapt to the wheel-house door to find Chico desperately hanging onto the steering compass with one hand and clutching his throat with the other. The wheel spun unattended.

'Senhor!' he gasped, his eyes rolling in the dim glow of the instrument illumination.

'Es no good! The sheep, it will not steer astraight. Oh, my head . . . !'

I burst through the curtain to the chart-room, reeling heavily myself as a fresh wave of fumes broke over me.

Johansen stood transfixed by the kettle, which was boiling away merrily. His eyes held a glazed expression. Next to the kettle stood the jug I had used that afternoon. It was half empty.

Johansen was boiling up my alcohol. One hundred per cent proof!

Savagely I tore the cable from the socket.

'Outside!' I roared.

It would only be seconds before the whole thing burst into flames and, with the fumes about, most of the bridge as well. Johansen woke up and rushed for the door. I followed him out, grabbing Chico on the way.

Doulos performed a slow circle on the face of the waters as the whole of the bridge watch crouched in the open at the extreme corner of the starboard wing.

Nothing happened.

After the second circle I ventured, carefully, back into the chart-room. The kettle and contents were intact. I breathed a prayer of thanks and ordered Johansen to take the wheel. He shambled, shamefaced, to obey.

'I thought it was water,' he moaned.

'Which comes out of a tap,' I continued severely, for we had returned from the brink of disaster and I was still shaking with relief at our escape. 'Next time make the effort to go and get it.'

Poor lad, not only did he have me to contend with, but the captain would also want to know what had happened to his ship's main magnetic compass. He would be unlikely to have a very bright morning.

I found Chico outside, sobering up in the blast of air that came over the dodger.

'What I need badly,' I opened, as I joined him, breathing in deep draughts of cool sea air, 'is a cup of very black coffee. Perhaps you'd like to make it for us tonight, eh, Chico?'

11
Brazil — and Danger

The fog clung round the bridge like a winter cloak, hanging
and touching, but with none of the warmth. The bridgewing
doors were, of necessity, open to enable sounds, such as the
sudden booming of a fog horn, to be heard both inside and out,
and the clammy air settled, chilly, on both skin and clothes. It
formed a dewy bloom on compass and binoculars, making
them slippery, unfriendly. And the menace of not being able
to see sent a moist trickle down our spines as well.

Religiously, our ship's whistle sounded out, hooting into the
night, fearing an urgent reply. The mysterious and invisible
radio beam from the radar scanner fingered the horizon as a
blind man feels carefully around him in a strange and foreign
place.

We were making another landfall: Cape Hatteras, sometime
graveyard of Atlantic voyagers. Low, marshy, backed by inland
lakes and waters and often, as now, haunted by off-shore mists,
it gives no inkling of its presence until you are right upon it.
Even radar is of little help, for the very flatness of the coastline,
with its backdrop of lagoons and sands gives scant response on
the screen until it is close aboard.

Compounding our problem was the fresh and vigorous Gulf
Stream current, fairly whistling up along the coast, delighted
to be free from the motherly constraints of the Florida Straits
and eager to show off its adolescent strength before dissipating
tepidly in the grey and restless waters of the North Atlantic.

We had been able to take no star sights at sunset, though our
noon fix was good, so I had been able only to guess at the spate
of the stream, wild and unpredictable in its geographic youth.

For all my navigator's art, I too could only join the captain
and officer of the watch in a ritual procession round the bridge:
peer into the radar hood, grunt, move back and inspect the

chart, step out into the soggy blackness, lift the binoculars, sweep the night and listen. The drone of our own siren. Back to the radar . . .

Then, an angel smiled. The shifting, tenuous fog-bank lifted and rolled on, and, before the next could claim us we saw a flash, way over to port. The beckoning beam of America, Cape Hatteras light. A quick bearing and we had a fix. We were further to the north than expected – the current was showing off tonight – but we were comfortably off shore and clear of any dangers. Smiles and conversation.

Taking a number of bearings, we swung round onto our approach course for Chesapeake Bay and I went below. Having found America for them, it would be nothing to do with me if they lost it again. But, although the fog returned, as I discovered when I came on watch later, we had the land firmly nailed to the radar screen and the occasional swirl in the mist revealed an appropriate lighthouse or two as confirmation.

At dawn, on a suddenly clear morning, we steamed proudly into Newport News, USA, one of the greatest naval ports in the world.

Spread before us was the most massive concentration of floating fighting hardware I had ever seen. Grey-painted hulls were everywhere. On quay after quay, trot after trot, double- and even triple-banked on the jetties, the warships filled every nook and cranny of the harbour – and the anchorage as well – each sporting its own collection of guns, missiles, antennae and energetic deck-party of sailors. The whole place was humming, bustling, whistling and bugling, with tugs and tenders hurrying about, cranes clattering and hooting – and ourselves apparently caught in the middle of this maelstrom.

Our pilot, however, was far from concerned.

'Welcome to America, captain,' he yawned as he mounted the bridge. 'Lucky you've caught us on a quiet day.'

But he led us to a peaceful corner of this vast seatropolis, to a berth where the boulevards touched the river bank and the autumn leaves of Virginia drifted down onto the placid, if slightly cloudy waters. We sent our lines out, moored, and I caught the next plane home – literally: it left six hours after the first rope hit the quay. Even the purser was amazed at his own efficiency.

Doulos was light-years away when I stepped out onto the rain-dampened tarmac of Gatwick airport the next morning and took a train to the friends' house where Elizabeth was staying. Richard already seemed much better. Within a few weeks I had obtained work on the bridge of a cross-channel ferry and we had moved into a rented cottage in the beautiful weald of Kent. God, it seemed, had been making some arrangements in our absence. Soon he was putting in overtime, for we were blessed (or was it blasted?) by the first cries of baby Timothy who arrived the following year, along with the very good news that I had successfully passed my examinations for 'Certificate of Competency as First Mate of an Ocean Going Vessel'.

But blessing usually brings responsibility, so I was not entirely surprised one morning when a letter plopped into our letter-box bearing the postmark and colourful stamps of a South American republic. It was headed: Ship's Office *MV Doulos*. Elizabeth was not surprised either, though, to do her justice, her emotions centred more on the contents than the fact of its arrival.

'If you think,' she started coolly and levelly, letting the paper find its own place amongst the breakfast cups, her brown eyes flashing dark and dangerous, 'that at the whim of some dreaming ship director I'm just going to pack my bags, hoist a toddler under each arm, shut up a home that I am *just* getting used to and jet off round the world to settle in a broom cupboard on *that* old tub, you have another think coming!'

The decibels raised on the last word were enough to send our adopted farm cat streaking from the room in terror and to wake the goats dozing gently in the summer sun at the bottom of our garden. They bleated in friendly, if sleepy, support.

So it was that a few months later we found ourselves strapped into the reclining seats of a plane belonging to one of Britain's larger airlines, gazing down upon the rugged countryside of southern Brazil. Our destination, Sao Paulo – and *Doulos*.

St Paul, the first missionary traveller. In a sense we were adopting his lifestyle, for he too had traversed the seas for his Master. But he could never have conceived of the circumstances of our mission, nor the size of the city laid out below us, with a population approaching that of the whole Roman Empire of his day. Sao Paulo lays claim to being the fastest growing, if not the largest city in the world. It sprawled, a staggering conurbation, across the southern horizon.

Abruptly we turned and began our descent to the airport, some distance to the west. In fact *Doulos* was lying in the major coffee port of Santos, to the east and over 2,000 feet below the Sao Paulo plateau. We still had a three-hour coach drive ahead of us on landing. Brazil is a big country. We had had a night and morning in the air, and only half of that had been spent crossing the Atlantic.

Our arrival on board ship was unannounced before the event, as is normal with joining personnel. Arrangements may change, and hopes of reunion are better not raised if they are likely to be dashed. Greeting old friends therefore took the form of the shock-and-surprise approach. This has its good points, but after the tenth scream of delight, or possibly horror, it began to tell, especially on our much-travelled nerves. We were undoubtedly pleased to see everyone, but our 'broom cupboard' was what we wanted most of all.

Eventually the chief steward got word of our plight and showed us to our cabin. This time it proved to be in the bowels of the vessel, though still with a port-hole, much to Elizabeth's relief. We had also, wonder of wonders, a full sized pull-out double bed *and* our own shower and toilet. Next door was a small annexe with two bunk beds for the boys. It really was first-class accommodation. We deposited our suitcases, tucked up two bemused children, slid out our caravan style bunk and collapsed until the following morning.

At breakfast we were announced, being actually there in the flesh, and accorded the usual welcome of a round of applause. We felt at home immediately and friends came across to greet us – in a more gentle manner. I left Elizabeth to their, now tender, mercies, donned my working boiler suit and officer's beret (my normal daily rig from then on) and took a wander round, to greet the old lady herself.

She looked and felt different. Basically she had not changed, of course, but now she seemed to have organization and purpose. The kinks and bumps had been ironed out. I had left her a brand-new project, game but gauche. Now she had felt the weight of her harness for over two years and had measured her stride to the load. Specific, physical changes had been made which also transmitted this feeling to me.

The steering gear was new. Gone, sadly, was the huffing and puffing sauna bath of the early days. In its stead squatted a neat and efficient but lack-lustre electro-hydraulic replacement. It had been prayed for and, I understood, provided at the last refit. A special gift from some European supporters. I could see it was the very model of a modern steering system, but it lacked the warm, wheezy, spirit of the other (steam) system which had, after all, steered her safely through two world wars.

On the bridge, too, the old wood-and-brass wheel had been torn out, along with its staunch cast support, to be replaced with a weedy steel pillar on which reposed what must be politely described as a joystick. It certainly was not a wheel; it resembled most closely the twin antennae of an over-large ant. It clicked delicately back and forth under the little finger of the helmsman and the rudder followed suit. Enough! It did the work, and most excellently too.

Allied to this, and very useful, if no more attractive, was an automatic pilot, designed and built on board by the electronics department. This meant that, at sea, we could dispense with the helmsman completely. The ship would steer her own course. In harbours and close waters we would, for safety, put a 'man on the wheel', but otherwise on passage it would click away to itself, adjusting the rudder, its electronic mind presumably thinking the same thoughts and dreaming the same dreams as all the previous, human helmsmen had conjured over the years — and possibly a few more besides.

These were major changes, and there were others. There was a new book lift for number two hatch — no more plunging through the dining saloon flooring to gain access there. And there was a second radar set, stabilized with the compass – a superb set, though not new – really vital for safe watchkeeping. I was very pleased. But most of the changes were in more subtle, minor improvements – re-rigging the derricks, re-design of the carpenters' workshop, completion of the book and cassette library for the crew, and so on.

I had a wonderful time nosing around and finding out. The offices – new typewriters and headed paper. Holds and bookstores – computer terminals, safety fire doors. Hospital, laundry, welding workshop, recording studio and electronic control room – lighting, work benches in wood and steel, power points, new tools. The list went on and on, and so did I. When the lunch gong sounded, it caught me still in working clothes. I took lunch in the mess-room, with the deckmen and engineers, who could eat together there and save changing until the day's end. An extraordinary cross-section of the world's races met me over the meal. Once again I faced the food – and an extraordinary cross-section of the world's ingredients also remade their impact.

The port of Santos lay on a river and its short estuary. The whole of the north bank, in fact, comprised the wharfage of the port. This ran for two or three miles and, from our berth, we could look down along a near-solid line of ships towards the bend in the river which greeted the sea.

Hardly had one ship discharged its cargo than another, already anchored in the bay, slipped in to take its place in the line. The air was full of the sound of thudding crates, clattering tackle and the shouts of dock labourers.

Behind the double line of warehouses which fronted the wharves lay the city itself, low and uncluttered, except for one distinctive hill which rose from the centre, as if to show the tall mountain ranges across the river that it could still do something in opposition. The small, but frantically busy, shopping centre slipped into the suburbs, with open-fronted emporia spilling out onto the street, and buzzing covered markets which must rate as some of the most attractive in the world for colour and display.

Strange and exotic fruits – passion fruit, papaya (paw-paw), giant avocado (big as a rugby ball, would you believe?) – jostled with more familiar melon, orange and banana, almost eager to spring into your basket. They did, too, for the prices were pence only. Our small 'allowance' for incidentals went a very long way in Santos (we were permitted to use about £2 a week each, from any gifts sent to the ship for our benefit).

Straight through the city centre from the wharves was the wide, open beach of hard-packed sand which, with the river, set the limits of urban growth within watery boundaries. But across the estuary climbed the mountains and massive interior of the country. Sao Paulo first, soon familiar, then other names: Campinas, Belo Horizonte and Brazilia. They were hundreds of miles inland but, compared with the deep interior to the north – the Amazon basin – no more than cities on a coastal plain. Feeding these cities – and especially Sao Paulo – from the south was our present port.

Day after day, up the steep mountain motorways an endless stream of heavy lorries would grind and jerk their way inland, leaping from peak to peak across magnificent gorges, bridged by spidery suspensions, dragging the dismembered cargo of hundreds of ships to the hungry giant of the heights. Like a greedy Gulliver in Lilliput the metropolis demanded more and more freight-loads, swallowing them up and sending the trucks back down the mountainside again, rattling and swaying, only on condition they returned the next day with more.

We discovered much about Brazil in those first days, not least that it was dangerous. A multi-racial society with no hang-ups about black or white – but, with people drawn from southern Europe and Africa down the generations, fair hair marks one down immediately as a foreigner, most likely rich and American, certainly fair game for knife or gun-point robbery.

The lovely beaches are safe, provided a group stays together, bathes in twos and leaves nothing on the sand. But it was wise always to keep a weather eye open and be prepared to move fast if a gang of men seemed to be heading your way. Mindful of this we took precautions. Even so, within a week of arriving, we were in for a shock.

Elizabeth had taken Richard and Timothy ashore for a walk. A busy ship is a restricting place for young children. Wisely, she thought, she would stay within sight of the ship and the customs post at the dock gate. The entrance to a small canal, for the use of ferryboats, was cut through the quayside, with a bridge spanning it for communication along the wharves. Richard had run on ahead a little way and had just reached the parapet when a man stepped out from the parked cars on the far side. He grabbed him firmly by the arm.

Elizabeth smiled gratefully at him. 'Obrigado,' – 'Thank you.' She could see he had been concerned for the child's safety.

The man did not reply but tightened his grip on the boy and breathed heavily.

Elizabeth smelt an uncouth mixture of sweat and spirit. Her smile froze on her lips and a quiver of fear ran through her. The man leered at her and jerked Richard towards the canal.

'Dinheiro,' he spat – 'Money.' Elizabeth's eyes widened as she realized the implication of his threat. If she did not give him the money, he would roll Richard into the water. She could see he was drunk enough to do it, too.

But she was not the tourist he thought. She had only a few cruzeiros, a matter of pence, on her. She spread her hands to indicate her plight.

The man grunted and jerked Richard sharply. He did not believe her.

In horror, Elizabeth motioned again. She had no money. Look, he could see.

Her wrist-watch flashed with the desperate motion and his eyes fastened on that. It had been a gift from me on her birthday.

Holding Richard with one hand he reached out and grabbed her arm, tearing at the strap. It sprang loose and he let go of the child.

Elizabeth dived for him, wrenching the boy free while he was holding the watch and, before he could respond, started running back along the quay to the safety of the ship. Timothy, oblivious of the drama, gurgled excitedly in his push-chair.

Nearby, a customs guard eyed her hurrying figure coolly, tapping his side-arm. Robbery was no business of his. Tourists had it coming to them, they could afford it.

Thankfully, Elizabeth reached the safety of the gangway.

I knew nothing of the incident until half-past six when, deck-work finished, I went down for tea. I found her furious – mainly with herself at having been caught out.

She spelt out the story in between ramming mouthfuls of baby food into Timothy's somewhat surprised countenance. She was furious with herself, for not 'standing up' to the man, furious with the officials for doing nothing, and above all furious with God for dropping her into all of this. She indicated the 'this' with a vicious arc of carrot purée and baby spoon. Most of the dining saloon was included.

I maintained a low profile, skulking behind a range of jam jars, until the explanation was over.

'Well, I think you did jolly well,' I ventured encouragingly.

She fixed me with a sizzling stare.

'Don't you patronize me, Clive Langmead. Don't you dare!'

'All right. If you want it from the top: Jesus told us to love our enemies and right now you don't seem to be doing too well with your friends!'

She gave me a hard look. We continued eating in silence for several minutes.

'I'm grateful he didn't let me lose my head,' she murmured, 'and Richard . . .'

I felt her hand reaching out underneath the table. I took it in mine and gave it a firm squeeze.

'I know you are, my love, I know you are.' God had been with her despite appearances, I was sure of that.

'Oh, Clive,' she sighed, looking away, her gaze now sad and troubled. 'Jesus lost more than a watch, didn't he?'

He had, which was one of the reasons why we were there.

Naturally I had to report the event to the Captain, who re-emphasized the stern warnings that had already been issued to the ship's company about safety and security ashore.

We, as a family, instituted our own shore-going policy. It was mainly a matter of dress, and we called it the throw-away look.

All the clothes we wore ashore could readily have been thrown away.

I obtained a pair of faded jeans which I secured with a length of heaving-line as a belt, a T-shirt which looked as though it had been used at that meal in the ape-house at Chessington Zoo and a pair of rustic sandals, bought locally. Elizabeth had a slightly more feminine equivalent, and Richard was told to dress himself just as he pleased – which was guaranteed to produce the required down-market effect. We also removed our wedding rings before leaving.

The only thing we could not change was the beacon of fair hair, mainly the children's. Short of buying wigs, there was little we could do. Hats would not stay on and anyway they were as distinctive as the hair itself. It was a continual source of interest to the Brazilians, on the beach or in the street, and many would go out of their way just to pat or feel its texture. We could not stop this of course, but we always felt uneasy about being singled out in this way.

Happily we had no more trouble for the rest of our stay. What we were taken for is anyone's guess, but we left snappy dressing to the locals from then on in.

A couple of days after, the captain (the gentlemanly American whom we had known, but not sailed under, before) phoned me on the bridge as I was running through some chart corrections.

'Say, I'd like you to come down here a moment, Clive.'

'Ah, right away, sir.'

I entered his cabin and took the offered chair. He opened a drawer in his desk and took out a small parcel.

'I can't tell you how this got here, Clive, but on behalf of myself and the ship, this is for Elizabeth, with our love.'

It was a lady's wrist-watch.

Elizabeth still wears that reminder of her first few days in Brazil, a country she, and all of us, learnt to love, not hate, despite the unwelcome greeting, and from whose people and culture we were to receive so many more small gifts of love before we sailed on.

12

Man The Lifeboats

Rio. Rio de Janeiro. The city with the most romantic reputation in Latin America and surely the most beautifully set. Not that I felt all that romantic when called out of my warm bunk in the small hours to prepare for arrival there. But such is the sailor's lot, and nobly borne.

'Bye!' muttered Elizabeth smugly from under the blanket. But she missed a treat.

Rio is a natural harbour with a narrow entrance opening into a large and sheltered basin guarded by Sugar Loaf Mountain, which stands sentry to seaward. At dawn it was breath-taking.

The distant city, already astir, seemed to crouch tensely beneath its surrounding circle of mountains, their peaks catching the first coat of crimson gold, some stepping gracefully up and back to the far misty horizon, others blasting sharply skyward, like petrified space rockets, slender plumes of rock pointed with sharp pinnacles.

The most striking of these is The Corcovada. On its summit, the Christ with outstretched arms — replica of the statue in Lisbon — was brilliantly bathed in dawn red. Blood for a Redeemer. Then a flash of yellow. Golden honours for a King. We held no faith in a statue, but it was a dramatic and soaring reminder of the Son of man himself and stayed our thoughts on him for an eternal instant.

The light grew. Along the shore the beaches gleamed white with sand and surf. The smooth curve of the bay swooped away from each side of us as we passed the narrows. Sea birds wheeled out and called a welcome; the ferry from Niteroi did the same as it frothed past.

Rio, city of dreams, gateway to culture, mirror of Latin America.

My mind, thrilled by the excitement of it all – the possibilities, the rich and stylish promise – took wing to new heights of imagination and fastened on – beefburgers. I had heard there was a cheap burger bar near the quay. There is, after all, culture and culture. Being the most cosmopolitan of cities Rio had adopted the fast-food fad from the north with delight. Even fighting 120 per cent inflation (prices changed almost nightly), we found we could afford the occasional indulgence. Others, I know, have more pungent memories of Rio, jewel of the southern ocean, but to me those beefburgers were beautiful.

So, it must be said, were the people. Like all Latin peoples they took great pride in their personal appearance and had good dress sense.

In England we worry whether our borders are tidy, the grass mown or the kitchen properly decorated. A wisp out of place is only a serious fault if it falls from the fuschias, a colour clash a calamity only when it lies between curtain and carpet, an image amiss only when it arises from a mal-adjusted line hold.

With a Latin everything is personal. What they wear, when they wear it, whether it matches. Fashion rules with a firm, but flamboyant hand. Even jeans and sweat-shirts are carefully chosen, judged with shoes – even the lowly glitter-plastic sandles – baseball hats or hair-slides to produce a pleasing effect. Sometimes overly so.

'Oh boy, oh boy! These women sure dress to kill!' opined an exasperated engineer as we leant together on the rail one morning, watching the crowds assemble for another day of visits and conferences. Constrained as he was by his single status and the (voluntarily accepted) firm rules on board about dealing with the opposite sex – so many attractive young people being thrown together in such close confines – he was feeling a mite frustrated. An outspoken and open-hearted Australian, his choice to serve on board was costing him in a lot of ways I had not even begun to imagine, safe in the intimacy of my marriage.

It was not easy for any of the young people to forego, even temporarily, the natural powerful desires of youth in order to work out their faith in service to others. They were full-blooded men and warm-hearted, vital women. But they were also concerned to leave aside, for the time being, the sex and soda pop stage in relationships — on which so many of their contemporaries around the world were attempting to build hasty and doomed partnerships — and to reach down deeper to discover for themselves the real foundation stones of life.

It was perhaps the least recognized, but most constant miracle on board that these eager searchers were never, if they were sincere in their purpose, unsuccessful in their quest.

We berthed on a quay that overlooked the moorings of the Brazilian Navy's submarines — and many were the evenings that Richard and I would watch the shiny-wet whale-like hulls slip quietly back into their berths after a day on exercise. Not long after, I was piped to call at the information desk. This usually meant that some official from the port, or ships' chandler, was calling to check certain papers or canvass for our business. But, arriving at the counter, I was handed a message from the programme manager: 'A Brazilian businessman has just called,' it read. 'We know nothing about him but he has invited a family with children to go and stay with him in the mountains — somewhere called Petropolis.'

I dropped around to the programme office, the nerve-centre of the ship's dealings with the general public. Bellowing quietly to be heard above the clack of typewriters and jangle of phones — the place resembled the news-room of a busy Daily — I established that we had been chosen from a list of thousands to accept this invitation. (This meant that we had been the first family that sprang to mind.) Still, I was not complaining. Not everyone would have the chance to take a cool weekend break in the mountains — though the fact that the man was unknown concerned me a little. Perhaps we were going to be taken for a ride, in more senses than one.

In the event we had a great time. The businessman himself spoke good English and liked to talk, so we listened, mostly. Elizabeth did her best with his family in Spanish, which is not Portuguese but the nearest we could get, and the children just played together with instant understanding.

Petropolis, we found, was the Brazilian equivalent of Simla in British India: the place where the old imperial government (first Portuguese and later a monarchy) used to retire from the summer heat of the capital. The cool height of the mountains tempers the oppression of the December sun standing almost overhead in Rio. Now, it is a small market town. Its imperial splendour resides only in the old palace of King Pedro, a museum and tourist attraction. Ornamental gardens surround this intricate, arching and totally European building, with its mementos to the grandeur of the Portuguese Empire – as though fending off the modern and very practical Brazilian culture of today.

We saw nothing like it again until we visited a theatre in the major colonial foundation of the north: Belem. This too spoke of transplanted Europe. Oddly enough, although distinctive, neither looked entirely out of place, set on mountains or locked in jungles. But perhaps it is just that we Europeans, too, have a colonial legacy to remember.

At his home we ate, not beefburgers, but strong local dishes, rich and spicy. These were served by a maid and prepared by a cook, though our host was not an obviously prosperous man – he lived in a third-floor town flat. Meat, beans, rice. This was the basis, as it is for the whole of the country, with manioc in place of potatoes. For us it was cunningly prepared and served – for the poorer people the meat is cut out, and the fare simply rice and beans. We also tried some tiny bananas – the size of a finger – known as 'gold' from their orangy colour. They tasted like melted butter.

The climax of our weekend was a surprise invitation to witness a singing competition at a nearby church. What startled us was the loud shouting and cheering that greeted our own entrance. I was pushed up onto the stage to speak (I was also pressed most forcibly to sing, but since I felt warmly towards them I declined) and was cheered enthusiastically at every mention of the name of the ship or some detail of our work. It was a moving evening and the ability of the eventual winner of the competition would, I am sure, have rivalled that of many well-known names in the commercial music world.

How, I enquired of our host as we walked home through the warm, still streets of the town late in the night, had they known so much about us and our work, since the ship lay so many miles away?

'Ah, my friend, if you take so much trouble to come all this way to encourage our faith and understanding, we take the trouble to find out!'

It was deeply gratifying, then, to know personally that our efforts on *Doulos* were appreciated. Of course we knew this from reports – in general terms. But so much of the time I was meeting officials who were, quite understandably, suspicious and defensive.

Our cargo was unusual, our intentions strange, our requirements different from those of other ships with which they had daily contact. We were often misunderstood, especially at the beginning of a port visit. A very unknown quantity. We had to earn the right to be treated normally, more often than not. But I have seen policemen and officials cheering, waving and even applying a surreptitious handkerchief when it came to sailing day, a couple of weeks later.

It was in Rio that I began to speak at meetings a little. Mostly this was in local churches, to many of which large numbers of the crew would be invited each Sunday. Dressed in our best we would meet in small groups, or teams, at an appointed time. One would bring a guitar, another make some notes so that he could explain how he became involved with the ship, or perhaps mention some customs from his own land which might interest a congregation (who, in all probability, had never met a Swede or a Malaysian before) and I, because of my famous linguistic ability, would offer to speak.

Of course, I had to be translated. A church that could not provide a translator had to forego the delights of my brilliant delivery of the spoken word, my apposite phrase, my affectionate pun, my literary allusion – most of which did not bear translation anyway. One had to be very careful. It is very dangerous, for example, to assure an audience in Rio that one has come across many strange nuts in Brazil!

There is one advantage, however, to be gained from being translated (apart from the reduced necessity of note preparation – you need only half the time) and that is that the pauses while you wait for your golden thoughts to be transformed, present you with the ideal opportunity to think of something sensible to say next. Very valuable indeed. Now, of course, if I am ever asked to speak in English, the whole thing comes out like bursts of machine-gun fire as I subconsciously wait for the non-existent translator!

On board, however, as indicated in the ship's articles, my job was not star speaker but professional sailor and, addressing myself to my duties one day, I discovered that we were shortly going to run out of qualified lifeboatmen in the crew. Or, more correctly, lifeboatpersons.

Legally, to put to sea every ship has to have a minimum number of people especially trained in the use of the boats – how to launch, row and survive in them in case of emergency. Because of a number of special teams being sent inland and the movement of other personnel ashore I had noticed we would soon be below that number and therefore unable to sail. We would have to train and certify some more in a hurry.

I arranged to teach a one-week 'crash' course. Contrary to rumour, the 'crash' was intended to reflect the desired speed of learning rather than the effect on the lifeboat used for practice. Anyone was welcome to attend and some twelve did, including two from the programme office, a plumber, an electrician and a nurse from the hospital.

There was also Elizabeth.

On the first day I let them in gently. I smiled.

'G'morning and welcome to the Rio Lifeboat Course. You are reminded that you are here to live, breathe, think and sleep *lifeboats*. This week contains nothing except *lifeboats*. They will be your life and, *if you are not careful*, maybe your death! So *jump* when you are told to jump, look *lively at all times* and remember you *love lifeboats*!'

A pupil yawned in the back row.

'*Langmead!* What was I talking about?'

'Er, something about jumping, I think . . .'

'*Wrong!* I strongly suggest some of us begin to pay a little more attention, don't you?'

I could see I was going to enjoy this. In the mornings we were ensconced in the class-room loaned to us for the week by one of the (five) schools on board. But after lunch we launched faithful number two boat – running through the complete process of winding it in and out – and rowed round the harbour, submarines notwithstanding. Here the team acquired the rudiments of seamanship and boathandling, with a few blisters. I continued with my sensitive instructional technique.

'*Right*, lower away! *Langmead!* What do you think you are doing with that rope? You are securing a boat, not tying a shoelace!'

'Toss oars *together*! Come on Langmead, put some weight into it, you're not tossing a *salad*!'

'*Langmead*! I said keep the boat *straight*! Look at the wake, lady. If I'd wanted you to sign your name, I'd have given you a pencil!'

It really was going extremely well.

Yet somehow I sensed that our relationship – possibly due to pressure of work – had grown, well, a little cooler. Nevertheless, after the fourth day my patient tolerance bore fruit. Elizabeth's voice had acquired the clip and command of a latter-day Captain Bligh. The others were close behind. Each took it in turns to exercise the class under my benevolent gaze.

I looked down the life-jacketed line on the boat deck. I coughed.

'Launch number two boat! *Langmead*, take charge!'

'Launch number two boat, aye, aye, sir! Crew . . .*Number*! Numbers one and two in the boat, numbers three and four send out the painter, numbers five to eight unship the davit handles, number one check the drain plug, number two . . . *Silence on deck*!' She glared over the backs of the toiling crew at the idle group of spectators who had gathered to watch the fun as a sort of matinee entertainment.

The offenders cut their conversation instantly and looked nervously at each other, wondering at the sinister transformation that had overtaken the gentle spirit they had grown to love. What had come over her? They questioned with their eyes, not daring to speak. What dark shadow had crept across her transparent Christian virture, sweetness of nature, warmth of character? Was she, perhaps, beginning to crack under the pressures of life aboard? They did not know, but it was obviously safest to do as one was told.

With nary a hitch the lumbering craft inched slowly, but smoothly, from its cradle, swung out over the blue waters of the harbour and disappeared from view, dropping from boat-to embarkation-deck, two decks below, its progress indicated by loud commands, reports and responding shouts.

'. . . weight *on* the bowsing tackles . . . *slip* the tricing pennants . . . Number two boat lowered and ready for embarkation, SIR!'

The voice floated up to me on the boat-deck. I lifted a quizzical eyebrow and leant over the ship's side.

'Toggle painter a bit slack, gripes should have been stowed inboard, otherwise quite good.'

Elizabeth glowed. 'Oh, thank you darl . . .'

'Carry *on*, Langmead!'

I was too far away to hear her, rather soft, reply.

Friday dawned, the day of the examination. It was run as the training had been: theory in the morning and practical in the afternoon.

'How much drinking-water does an inflatable life-raft carry? How would you rig the sea-anchor? What use is the steering-oar?' (The answer is not: You may well ask.)

The questions I fired were endless. But they had all done their homework and the answers were ready. They all passed. I was not so surprised. Whatever people were asked to do on *Doulos* they did it with full enthusiasm. They wanted to pass and, with a little help from me, took the trouble to see that they would.

I had actually run a similar course for a *Doulos* group in London during our previous trip. Then I had been up against the salty expertise of the Master Mariners from the Department of Trade. They grilled my candidates. All had passed on that occasion as well, much to the incredulity of the examiners — and to me!

I was very satisfied. But then I came up against an unexpected problem. No one from the Port Authority was available to sign the certificates. No signature, no validity, and if we could not show the requisite number of certificates to sail . . .

I telephoned office after office in the Port Administration building, trying to find someone who would rubber-stamp and sign the forms. I had to work through an interpreter, of course, and this made it all the more frustrating. I could not tell if the girl was explaining it right. I drew a complete blank, from the port captain down.

Dejected, my mind went back to a disappointing conference I had recently been asked to lead on board. It had been arranged for members of the armed forces. A large group had promised to attend, but in the event only about ten people had turned up. It had been most embarrassing, but I had gone on with the show anyhow. I felt it would have been a pity to disappoint those who had bothered to come. I had made my message as constructive as possible under the circumstances, putting in a sharp mental note to God about my dissatisfaction at the situation. Very poor, I thought.

When I had finished, one of the visitors came over to thank me for the effort. He introduced himself as a naval engineer, a man of strong faith with a deep interest in the project. He gave me his card. If there was anything he could do . . . I felt it unlikely, but thanked him all the same.

Now I wondered . . . I searched out the card and returned to the telephone. I knew the man could speak English, so I avoided the translator.

'Ministry of Defence? Senhor Bocasio please. Ah, *Commander* Bocasio, yes, of course.'

'Hello, my friend?' His warm, accented voice greeted my enquiry. I explained the problem.

'Ah, you should have come to me before. The port captain is a good friend of mine. Send in your examination results and forms, they will be signed.'

Just like that. And they were – delivered by special courier to the ship the next day. I made a few apologies to the Almighty later on, I might add. It was humbling to think that he had concerned himself with my simple admin. problem, as well as the staggering cost and logistic support of the operation as a whole. Personal service indeed. Not everyone's wife has a lifeboat certificate signed by the port captain of Rio de Janeiro, now do they?

'Darling?'

'Mmm?'

'I never quite understood that bit about casting off . . .'

'Ah, well, what you need is some personal tuition.'

'That's what I thought, but no more noise, huh?'

'OK, now where would you like me to start?'

'There's no answer to that.'

But there was.

13
Wet Baggage

Gradually we worked our way northward along the coast of Brazil. Vitoria, a smaller port, followed next. It had beauty also, in a more charming, friendly style than the formal set piece of Rio. The entrance was along a river gorge, the steep cliffs concealing it effectively from the sea. The berth, right in the town centre, was some three miles inland. So steep were the sheer rock walls and so close did we come to them that the tugs had no room to secure until we were directly opposite the river frontage of the town. It was most spectacular, but without the broad grandeur of the two previous ports. Prior to berthing, our arrival had aroused some interest in the roadstead, off shore, mainly due to the repeat performance we had been forced to give when anchoring to await the pilot.

Approaching the rather busy anchorage from seaward, we had arrived very neatly over the predetermined, and possibly only, spot with enough clear swinging-room for us to stay, when the engineers phoned up to say, awfully sorry and all that, but they couldn't stop the jolly old engine. Would we mind steaming round in the odd circle or two while they had a crack at sorting it out?

The captain tactfully emphasized that they had not exactly chosen the most convenient time to discover such a fault. He was looking out through the wheel-house windows at the serried ranks of gently-dosing shipping through which we would now have to burst, Nelson-like, before reaching the comparative safety of the open sea. Fortunately, doing our best impression of the celebrated runaway train (coming down the track, hurrah) we managed to damage only the nerves of those luckless officers on anchor watch on the other vessels, and escaped, twisting and turning like a destroyer, to deeper water.

This manoeuvre aroused admiring comment from the

regular spectators below, who had concluded with some justification that we had smoothly executed a rather complex evolution, for some purpose unknown but no doubt important.

Further telephone exchanges between bridge and engine-room produced the assurance that the fourth engineer had traced the fault and that it would not happen again. We turned about and proceeded once more into the bay.

The captain, however, was taking no chances. As we went round we stopped and even went astern on the engines two or three times, as a test.

This was treated with less enthusiasm by the embarked audience, since it did not involve flashing past anchored merchantmen with inches to spare. But it had the most volcanic effect on the other shipping, whose crews concluded to a man that, barring a typhoon, we were the most dangerous thing about on the high seas. Crowding on deck they hung, festooned, all over what seemed to them the safest parts of their own craft, eyes and binoculars glued to our knife-like bow, carefully following our now rather cautious approach.

Eventually we made it. The Captain stopped the engine very early and we crawled into position with the last dying throw of the propellor. A burst of joy arose from the decks of the assembled shipping.

It was in Vitoria that we discovered Brazilian chocolate, which is extremely rich and more-ish, and playparks for the children, fenced and guarded but fun and friendly inside. We also, unexpectedly, came up against Latin American poverty at close quarters.

We had never closed our eyes to the poor of the country. They had been evident from our first day, through the windows of a city bus, in the streets next to a church, on the ship at a conference. (Anyone who wanted, could come.) But we had not seen them at home, in context, in the vast villages of shacks tacked onto the towns and cities like the diseased and putrefying sores, unhealed and untended, that clung to the limbs of beggars at street corners, exposed for our pity and disgust.

What we discovered was a Venice of the poor.

I had taken a lifeboat away for a trip up-river, as a recreational afternoon for some of the crew who had been putting in long hours over the past few weeks. Elizabeth and the children came too.

Initially we explored the various shallow and muddy tributaries that led off the main river. Finding a number of small islands we made a landing on one of them, but it was thickly overgrown and offered little more possibility for exploration than a short scamper along the shoreline. We pushed on upstream.

After a short distance the land flattened out and, with it, the river opened into a large lake. Another island stood in the middle. We circumnavigated this and then noticed, on the nearest bank, an area of habitation. We closed in to take a look at what we supposed to be an attractively-sited suburb of the town. But as we motored closer it became apparent that we were badly mistaken.

This was far from being a comfortable satellite of the metropolis. It was the unwanted *favella* or shanty town that had grown up behind. Furthermore, most of the dwellings were actually built in the water. Only a small section of the 'village' was founded on the bankside. Thin canes and poles supported the concentrated mass of irregular huts and hovels, formed from sections of corrugated iron, cardboard, ply pannelling – torn, not sawn – mud and reeds.

Between the tottering structures led wooden planks, like wheelbarrow runs at a building site, except that these were over water, not mud. Children, dark and lissom, leapt and darted from plank to plank and thence to the catwalks that led to the shacks themselves, occasionally, but not often, slipping and falling into the water beneath.

I cut the engine and we drifted in. Watery streets – for boats, or at least canoes – could be discerned between the huts, the planks did not bridge every gap. But my concern for our exposed propellor, and the strong stench that came from the commune, disinclined me to close it further.

The water was used, quite obviously, for all needs. From drinking and washing to cooking and, as it seemed to suggest most strongly, sanitary disposal. Whether or not it was a source of food as well, either there or out in the lake, I do not know. Apart from the canoes there seemed little evidence of effective fishing-equipment, though perhaps these poor could not afford such things, or were landsmen by background, living over the water simply through force of circumstance.

At the beat of our diesel a few people had drifted languidly out of their entrance holes – one could hardly dignify the construction by calling it a doorway – and stood, or sat squatting, gazing dully at our fresh-scrubbed faces and gleaming boat.

The gulf that divided us was not 100 yards of murky water, nor even 100 miles come to that. We were worlds apart. The rich and the poor. I, for all my much-vaunted sacrifice of income and security, was still incomparably richer than they. Each could not even conceive of the lifestyle of the other, we could never meet or touch or communicate. We were like alien invaders from another dimension, another galaxy, a different universe.

But that was not quite true. During our stay some of them did manage to make the journey across the town to the ship and come on board. Some of them heard about the poor, rejected craftsman from the despised slum-town of Nazareth. They knew what he felt, had suffered what he suffered. They understood him. And once they had met Jesus, we discovered that all of us had something to talk about, together.

But if the evils of poverty became apparent to me in Vitoria, evil itself waited for us at our next port: Salvador. Salvador looked and felt like a decapitated Gibraltar – the rock without its peak. It was a great promontory of stone thrust out into the sea, enclosing a harbour and supporting a fortress and ancient battlements for its defence. An impressive city, rather than beautiful. It was the first landfall for the Portuguese explorers and the base for their early administration of the fledgling colony 400 years ago. It was also acknowledged world-wide as the centre for 'Spiritist' worship.

I didn't need to be told that something was strangely amiss in the spiritual atmosphere. I could feel it. But surely, I must be joking? You can't feel spirits, let alone the atmosphere they leave lying about. Perhaps I had been partaking too much of another type of spirit? Maybe, on a bookship, I had been reading the wrong books, too late into the night? Well, maybe.

I only know that we all felt it, from the moment we berthed to the moment we sailed. Oh, in a simple sense we had a splendid time in Salvador. The officials could not have been more welcoming, we even had a band to welcome us in. We found a superb, sandy beach a short bus ride from the ship, the food improved, briefly, thanks to cheap vegetables and fruit, and a special consignment of books arrived by container, intact and on time. No, there were no complaints.

Why was it, then, that I felt an urgent need to rise early to go to the 5.30 a.m. prayer meeting on board? Why did we all feel that there was a thin, but insidious fog clamped down over the ship? Why the air of menace all about? Why the unexpected and irrational bickering that seemed to break out and needle its way amongst the crew, their wives and families? Every task in the day seemed a battle, every problem insurmountable, every imposition the last straw.

Evil? Yes. Personal? Yes. Very possibly Evil himself. I would not know. I certainly caught no sight of a trident or cloven hoof. But that would have been fun, naughty and laughable. This was sinister, heaving and oppressive, like a summer evening before the crash of a thunderstorm, or the leering calm before the blast of a tropical hurricane. But no tempest broke to clear the air and freshen the senses. Whatever it was, it brooded horribly over the city, drawing life and substance from those who served and worshipped it.

This was done quite openly. It was no surprise to walk the streets and see little parcels of food, flickering candles and an inverted cross or dark religious portrait set under a tree or monument, invoking aid for some domestic crisis, some personal problem or illness. And they would receive it, healing even, at times. But at what cost? To be absorbed into a twilight world, the soul in tether, the mind in chains.

Jesus was no fool. His insight was more penetrating than any man's.

'Do not fear,' he said, 'one that can kill your body, but rather he that can devour your soul.'

In Salvador, I fear, the meal is well into the second course.

We continued northwards, this time for our longest coastal passage between Brazilian ports. For five days we trundled on past the blank and featureless coastline, sometimes pulling way off shore to avoid outlying reefs, navigating by the stars, though following the line of the land.

Although I dislike figures intensely I have learnt to love astro-navigation – position-finding from the heavens. There is something very satisfying about standing outside on the wing of the bridge, with the sea swishing past and the deck gently lifting beneath your feet, your hair whipped smartly against your forehead in the blast of air, and holding the sextant up, steadily, to the steel knife-edge of the horizon. Slowly as you adjust the mirror, the floating green ball of the sun (eye-shades dim its brilliance and change its colour) settles uncomfortably on the still-visible line. Continuous manipulation keeps it there, sunset at midday, all done by mirrors.

'Stand by!' I shout to the time-keeper in the chart-room.

He gazes earnestly at the sweeping second-hand of the ship's chronometer. One more twist and the bouncing, irritable, ball is where I want it.

'Stop!' I touch the instrument no more. The time-keeper is busy writing down the exact time, to the second, of my cry. That, and the altitude now locked on the sextant, is the raw data for my calculation. I open my workbook and pore over tables and almanacs, scribbling figures and talking fussily to myself as I twist and tangle them in minor calculation.

A few minutes' work and I exhale a long breath. I have a line to plot on the chart. One sight, one line. I must take at least three, at a good interval, to find our position. A morning's work.

At dawn and dusk things move a little quicker, for the stars lie at different angles, and they must all be caught before they are too dim, or the horizon is too dark. Six stars usually mean a brisk ten minutes in the half-light (six gives a good margin for error). For speed I usually shout the star and elevation from outside. They have some jaw-cracking names:

'Stand by! "Betelgeuse" . . . stop! Fifty-four, thirty-three point six!'

'Fifty-four, thirty-three point, er, six!' The figures echo back at me from the chart-room port-hole.

'Stand by! "Rigel Kent" . . . stop! Twenty-eight, twenty-two point three!'

'Stand by! "Aldebarran" . . . stop! Thirty-five . . .'

The poor time-keeper has writer's cramp at the end of it. Twenty minutes later, calculations complying, the chart has plotted on it six pencil lines, converging nicely at a point. Well, nearly at a point. Usually it looks more like a rough sketch-map of Clapham Junction, but a general trend is discernible. A position within a mile is accepted. I make sure they always cross within a mile.

It was off this remote coast, in the early hours of one morning during my watch, that we began to sink.

The first I knew about it was a phone call from the night watchman. This was a deckman who patrolled the ship at night, checking the companionways, holds and store-rooms for fire, secure stowage and general safety. It was not actually in his brief to stand on the fo'c'sle every hour and cry out, 'Oyez, oyez, two bells and all's well!' But that conveys the idea.

'Bridge, first officer!'

'Ah, serr, night watchman here.' It was Enrico taking his turn tonight. 'Serr, I think we have a leetle problema in the baggage locker.'

'Yes, well, what sort of problem?'

'Es, ah, full of water, serr!' I stopped for a moment to let this sink in. The baggage locker, despite its name, was actually a very large space, forming most of the lower hold of number three hatch − the largest hatch, and bookstore in the vessel. We kept all our empty luggage there.

'Full?'

'Well, OK, half-full. All the cases are, ah, floating around inside.'

The picture was not encouraging. We were talking of flooding in tons at least.

'Watch it, Enrico. I'll see what I can do.'

I dialled the engine-room, always a ready source of help in time of trouble.

'Can you put suction on number three lower hold bilge?' I quizzed the voice that answered.

'Er, is this a broadly-based, general-interest enquiry, or is there something I should know?' came back the second engineer. I filled him in.

'Could be tricky, all those boxes and things. Might gum up the works,' he opined.

'Well, we'll just have to sink then, I guess.' I thought this might help, being a sensitive sort of person myself.

'I will give it a try,' he replied, rather frostily. Good as his word, he started pumping out. Unfortunately, being a man of experience in these matters his forebodings proved correct. Within minutes something had spread itself across the suction pipe, effectively blanketing the pump. Bravely, however, he made his way down to the hold and, after messing around for some time in the ever-deepening water, located the source of the trouble.

Part of the salt-water sanitary main, the pressurized piping used to flush the toilets, had burst just as it entered the locker. We were busy pumping seawater into our own hold! Quickly he shut down the sanitary pump and closed the valves. Now no one could use the toilets, but at least we would stay afloat. I could say he reported his achievement to me flushed with success, but since I could not see him that would be untrue.

The next morning came the great dry-out, as dozens of woeful crew members laid out their warped and soggy cases in the sunshine, us included. Many of them were unusable, having been adrift too long. Some of the crew had been keeping warm clothes, or old books and notes in their luggage and they had taken little liking to a castaway existence.

The decks resembled a jumble sale on a wet day. Most colourful of all were the Christmas decorations belonging to one family which had escaped the worst of the flood and were hung out round the poop. The children were disappointed to learn that the festive season had not yet arrived.

With the baggage removed, we managed to pump out the water quite quickly and repair the pipe, restoring toilet water to the ship – which was deeply appreciated. It only remained for me to commend the industry of Enrico in doing such a thorough job on his rounds. The access to the locker was always securely padlocked and his extra trouble in checking had saved us from a much more serious plight. I know of many professional seamen who would not have bothered.

Flooding aside, we made a good passage, following the stars, and an easy landfall at the pilot station, a desolate outpost on a similar coast, just on the lip of a great river. Salinopolis – salt town – that about said it all. Most of the shoreline around it on the chart was indicated by pecked lines: 'Not properly surveyed.' There were also such things as 'breakers reported here' and 'shoal patches likely' littered about. It gave one a great feeling of confidence. There was nothing to say 'here be dragons', but if no one had been out surveying I suppose nobody had met any.

We embarked the pilot and promptly left sight of land again as we proceeded the 100 or so miles upstream to our destination, Brazil's city of the north – Belem, gateway to the most famous river in the world, the Amazon.

14

Fireworks and Firefighters

Belem is actually situated on the River Para, which slots into the Amazon about 150 miles upstream. All shipping intending to make the additional 500-mile river passage up to the freshwater port of Manaus has to swap pilots at Belem, exchanging estuary for river guide. But we had no intention of threading our way through the jungle. Belem, apart from being the sea and air doorway to the whole river basin, was also the state capital and the largest centre of population. It was there that we wanted to be.

Unusually for a city port there were no tugs in Belem. This meant that all the berthing depended simply on the skill of the pilot and his judgement of the tides and winds, particularly using the strong current to swing the ship alongside her allotted berth.

Arriving during the late evening, we could only manage to find the last trickle of flood tide (the only one we could use – the ebb is too quirky). Thus we needed careful manipulation of our ropes, once we were opposite our designated hole in the line of ships, to 'warp' or pull alongside.

The ropes ran ashore with relative ease. There was, at least, a harbour workboat to carry them for us. But the delicate co-ordination required to heave simultaneously at both ends and give the odd burst on the engine was unexpectedly complicated by the sudden loss of communication from the bridge. The walkie-talkies were tuned, apparently, to the same frequency used by the local taxi company, a worthy outfit no doubt and well drilled in the economic use of words on the air, but with forty or so cabs on the road the captain's executive instructions were almost continuously drowned out by drivers demanding the exact address of their next fare, or ten minutes off for a coffee break.

The recourse to telephones, masterminded by myself, proved only a partial success. Jeff, down aft, found he had to keep one of his busy mooring-party permanently stationed in the laundry, where, amongst the dangling socks and steaming underwear, he could answer my calls dialled on the automatic exchange and relay the message to the poop.

Forward, the mate could only resort to the sound-powered version on the fo'c'sle, which was so quiet it demanded more decibels than Concorde to carry any message at all. I spent some of the time dangling from the bridge dodger with a megaphone, in an attempt to improve things, but he got fed up with the sepulchral voice booming instructions out of the lofty darkness, to which he could make no effective reply and I was forced to return to the hand-crank and holler.

Pilot: 'Heave in a bit more forward now, captain.'

Captain: 'Heave away easy on the head lines.'

Myself: 'Heave easy the head lines, aye, aye!'

I pick up the period hand-set, spinning the handle.

'FO'C'SLE, BRIDGE HERE! HEAVE AWAY EASY ON YOUR HEAD LINES! YES, YOUR HEAD LINES! NO . . . HEAVE! I . . SAID . . . HEAVE!'

For the sake of (my) throat and (others') eardrums it was a glad moment when we could 'ring off main engines', indicating that we had formally arrived.

Elizabeth loved Belem. The rich scent of the jungle, which crept down to the water's edge, seeming to invade the city with its omnipresent depth and mystery. The gentle Indian population so different, with their measured view of life, from the slick, hard-edged European stock further south. The comparative safety of the streets – one could walk short distances alone at night without fear. The rich cornucopia of the local market, overflowing with fresh forest fruit: quite literally, one stepped in quite a lot of it. The handicraft and cloth salesmen, the wide sweep of the muddy yellow river 1,000 miles from its source. It was an exotic place.

Further down from our berth lay the fishing-wharves. The fishermen worked the wide river estuary as they would a deep-sea catching-ground, such was its scope and size. They returned to Belem to market their haul. Naturally the dock attracted the attention of the bird population, and one day we wandered along to see the traditional fishing-scene.

When we came up to it Elizabeth gave a little squeak of horror, pointing to the wheeling and dipping scavengers, for they were not the familiar gulls that we had seen so often on the British coast, but vultures straight from the tropical rain forest, cawing and cackling and bobbing their bald heads up and down as they savoured the fishy remains, like infernal witches over a ghastly meal. But they were friendly enough. Dead meat was their interest and not one of them so much as coughed at us when we, brave but fascinated, went as close as we dared to watch them feeding.

With verdant flora and fauna so close Elizabeth indulged her interest in plants and flowers. She had taken on the post, among other things, of ship's gardener. This meant that anything green in the public rooms was her province (except seasick sailors). She had worked wonders with the plants and flowers over the weeks that they had been in her care. Everyone swore that they looked up when she passed by.

Seeing the lush growths ashore, however, and mindful of the less luxuriant Caribbean ahead, she persuaded the captain's wife to join her in a market expedition to get something in for the coming months.

Mid-morning brought a curious sight. Two large bushes, a smaller one and a push-chair were noticed edging their way along the dockside. *Macbeth* come to life. Closer investigation uncovered the facts. Elizabeth and entourage, including Richard, had bought up most of the jungle market to decorate the ship.

It was all much appreciated. It was amazing the number of people who stopped her in her daily watering and tending to thank her for her work. The sea and steel make harsh demands on the senses and something green and growing comes as a real refreshment to the spirit, as well as adding beauty and softness to the spartan environment.

Our reception at Belem exceeded all our expectations. Not only were all our conferences full, but a number of them had to be run twice. One particular subject drew in enough people for three conferences. What was most interesting about these was that those who could not come in for the 'first sitting' had to wait patiently on the quayside for the second, perhaps an hour or more later. With three, they'd have waited for most of the afternoon before getting aboard. And they didn't go away. The subject? The Christian Family.

All in all it was a popular time. The numbers of visitors in all ports had always run to five figures, sometimes six. In Belem we hit our record: 11,639 in *one* day.

The added interest was partly due to the extra numbers of visitors to the city itself for a week-long festival, originally religious in intention and dedicated, at least nominally, to the Virgin Mary.

The chief of the local police department was direct:

'We get more knifings, robbings and rapes during the one week of the festival than we get for the whole of the rest of the year. Be warned!'

It was clear that, whatever the original intention, the Spirit of God did not find a welcome in too many hearts during the celebration. A sad reminder to us, perhaps, of the fate of Christmas in Britain.

But we did not have to go ashore to find trouble. It came to us. On the day of the big parade, as dusk fell, I, being officer of the day wandered on deck to watch the firework display that had been scheduled as the climax. In due course the roar of the crowd (which I was unable to see because of warehouses) indicated the approach of the procession. Sure enough, within minutes there was the whoosh and thud of a rocket, with the staccato crackle of smaller explosions.

The first burst nearly overhead, some way from the square where it had been launched. The breeze, quite brisk I noticed, had carried it a long way down wind. As the bright golden shower faded I saw the spent case, glowing a dull red, fizzle into the river. It took me a second or two of idle contemplation to realize that it had landed in the water just down wind of the ship. In growing disbelief I followed the implications of my sharp observation: a slight fluke in the wind, a knot or two less in speed, and we would be under direct rocket attack! Chiming in with my thoughts came the reports of three more rockets from the square.

Clutching the rail, I watched desperately for the dim red-hot glow of the falling sticks in the glare of the burst. There was one, two – they would land on the quay. Where was the third?

Then I saw it.

It drifted lazily over the forward masthouse and settled sizzling on the wooden deck.

I clattered down the companionway, like a fireman answering the bell, grasped the stick by its unburnt end and threw it into the river. A small brown scorch-mark scarred the deck.

I rushed over to the watchman's post at the forward gangway, wrestling the phone from its stormproof mounting. I dialled a number, tapping the receiver impatiently as it rang. A voice answered.

'Bosun? Meet me on the captain's deck with as many men as you can muster in two minutes. Move!'

By rights I should have called out the full fire-party. Such a group was always ready on board, trained to respond. But an announcement, or even the sight of a hose-party forming up, accompanied by the rush and bang of the rockets, could be enough to start a panic on the crowded decks. Better to move quickly and quietly, if we could.

Seconds rather than minutes later came the sound of footfalls on the captain's deck ladder. It was the bosun, followed by Roberto, Toni and a half-dressed Sven. They emerged into the bulkhead light. I waved wildly at two burning embers sinking rapidly towards the area of number two hatch.

'Look! Put 'em over the side!' Sven and Toni scampered off.

There was another series of cracks in the sky and two more direct hits landed, glowing, on the place I had most feared: the book exhibition roof. Soft, rubberized (who knew how inflammable?), with painted wood panels.

'Roberto!' I hissed. Both he and the bosun darted forward, down onto the busy boat-deck thronging with people, then up again onto the unrailed, sloping roof that protected the exhibition area. Underneath, visitors browsing at the brightly-lit cabinets with their rows of shiny books, looked up in mild surprise at the muffled sound of running feet above their heads.

Roberto reached the hot remains. Kicking them into the water he stamped heavily on the slightly marred white roofing. One or two browsers decided reading gave them a headache. The bosun loped back to my position, arriving with a breathless Toni and Sven.

'All OK.' coughed Sven.

'Sure it isn't,' interjected the bosun, who had been watching the latest salvo straddle the ship.

'Down there, by the paint store!' he roared at the Swede, who was already running down the ladders and across the foredeck, elbowing his way through the visitors queueing by the entrance to the forward lounge.

The paint store!

Gallons of volatile liquid just waiting for a light. I would have to call out the fire-party, and take the risk. If it went up, the result would be too horrifying to contemplate. I turned to execute my thoughts, but the bosun laid a restraining hand on my shoulder.

'It's locked up,' he said. 'I checked.' I turned back, relieved. The rocket couldn't burn through a steel weather door. The bosun was a good man to have around in a crisis.

Sven reached the offending article and dropped it into the river. The danger had been real enough, though, for he reported that it had landed on a canvas winch-cover, which still showed signs of the encounter.

The bombardment lasted for a tense half-hour, but we got used to spotting the falling star behind the blaze of the explosion, and following it down to its destination on quay, river or deck.

We fielded them all.

Thanks to the quick action of the sailors we had avoided a serious accident. We all breathed a prayer of thanks when the banging ceased and the still night air flooded back across the parks and squares. We had undergone our baptism of fireworks.

In polite contrast to the wildness of the main festival an allied event, a series of classical concerts, was mounted in the central theatre, which, like the town of Petropolis, near Rio, had been constructed in the days of the Portuguese Empire. Maintained in its ornate glory as part of the national heritage, it was the ideal setting for both European and Brazilian music and dance. Members of the ship's company were offered a block of tickets, as a mark of thanks for our help to the community, and Elizabeth and I were able to attend on two occasions.

I know little of music and dance, but the memory of these hot, sultry evenings, with the carved verandah doors thrown open to the sky, the tinkle of the piano echoing round the gilded arches and the sounds of the city, river and jungle in the background is as evocative, to me, of the culture of Brazil as anything I can recall.

At last, loaded to the gills with plants, fruit, hand-crafted boxes, pottery, and – essential to survival in the tropics – a hammock (bought at a 'special' super-low price – I was hoping it wouldn't hang that way as well) family Langmead joined the rest of the crew in waving Belem, and Brazil, goodbye.

But the country didn't let us go without a struggle. On the morning of our scheduled departure a brisk wind sprang up and, being from the north-west, held us onto the quay. No tugs, remember.

The pilot came on board, took one look and advised us, in the strongest possible terms, to wait until the next tide. The captain demurred. We could not do that. Our schedule was tight. We, quite literally, could not afford to be late arriving in our next port.

We heaved in the offshore anchor we had left down for just such a contingency, hoping it would pull the bow out enough to catch the current. But the wind was too strong. It slid helplessly through the mud, coming home with an earthy clang. Now we had nothing to pull us against the wind. The pilot shrugged his shoulders. He had told us so.

The captain confronted him. Was there nothing he could do? No. Then he, the captain, would take over. The pilot shrugged again. He had met enough fools in his time; most of them had come to grief sooner or later.

'Right,' confirmed the captain, 'we'll spring her off.' I looked doubtful. We had ships immediately ahead and astern, leaving little room for fancy footwork.

'Oh, ah, aye, aye, sir,' was all I said. I had a word with Jeff.

'Could you let go everything except your "spring" and send out two more?' He confirmed that anything was possible – in the sort of voice one might have expected if I had asked him to dance the can-can on the poop-deck.

I asked the mate, forward, to let everything go as well. In a few minutes the snaking ropes had all retreated inboard from the quayside, barring three black-and-white strands, lying together, and leading from the stern to a shore bollard just over half-way along our length.

'Slow astern,' said the captain. The ship director, who had come to the bridge to enquire about the delay, bent his head, touching the dodger. Either he could not bear to look, or he was praying. I hoped it was the latter. With the thrust of the engine, if any one of those ropes gave, the two others would almost surely part and we would sink the ship astern of us. They were stretching, bar taut, already. If we stopped and they sprang back we would catapult into the ship ahead. The life of faith is never boring.

Jeff was singing out the distance of the ship astern as the propellor began to bite:

'Twenty feet and closing, fifteen, ten feet and closing, seven, five, still closing, three feet . . .' I stared at the captain, who was looking fiercely at the bow, willing it to leave the quay. 'One foot and closing, *minus* two feet . . .'

He had neglected to tell us that the ferry astern had a catamaran bow and we had backed between the two hulls! At last, miraculously, and I do not use the expression lightly, the bow moved slightly against the static superstructure of the ship ahead. It was lifting off! We looked again. Yes, a definite swing had developed. A ragged cheer broke out from the crowd on the quay. They could see the open water between us and the wharf. Suddenly there was daylight between the bow and the vessel ahead.

'Stop engine!' roared the captain. The tide had caught us and was pushing us further and further out. There was no time to be lost.

'Let go aft! Half ahead!'

The three ropes, their work done, went limp and urgent hands threw them off the bollard. They splashed into the water, but we dared not stop the engine now. Jeff and his sailors leapt on them and hauled them up desperately through the fairleads. The screw thrashed the river violently, sending a thundering cataract at close quarters under the twin hulls of the ferry.

We moved ahead. Another cheer from the assembled company ashore, followed by a tuneful rendering of 'Our God is good!' which faded slowly as we clawed our way clear of the dockside. Whether the crew of the ferry thought so, too, is open to debate, since we had no occasion to meet them after the incident. But *we* were grateful, that was for sure. For, although none of us would *swear* to seeing any angels pushing, starboard side forward, on departure, a number of us had a shrewd suspicion that they might just have felt in need of the exercise.

Over the horizon, the Caribbean beckoned.

15

Jewel of the Caribbean

As we steamed steadily north-west the familiar night sky of the northern hemisphere began to lift above the horizon. Once again the Pole Star, low on the starboard bow gauging our latitude, gave us a compass check in the dark hours, replacing the Southern Cross which had served us so well for the past months.

By day the colour of the sea, deepening to a more fiery blue, all the more noticeable to us, no doubt, because of the cloudy yellow of the Amazon outfall which we had just left, was the clearest signal to most people on board that the Caribbean was approaching. Offshore it had been blue, as against green for colder climes, for some time, but as we drew near the scattered daisy chain of the Windward Isles, it took on a glowing quality, sharing the colour from its own warm bosom, rather than stealing it from the cloudless skies overhead.

It was transparent, too, deep down. Dolphins, never far off, homing in like sleek torpedoes on our propellor noise, could actually be watched streaking below the surface or through the raised glassy wall of a wave as they darted from side to side, chasing around the bow or tumbling in the parting line of our wake. But even a modest twelve knots was too fast for long games and, in a matter of minutes, they would drop behind and plunge off to find another ship to tease.

Squadrons of flying fish (the national emblem of our destination) launched themselves continually across our path, skimming and flashing away over the wave-tops like shiny model airliners. Then one wave, higher than the rest, would reclaim them for their rightful element like a shower of hail, only to loose them again as our surging bulk pushed onwards in unintentional pursuit.

The air had lost the weight and humidity of the jungle and

was fresh, soft and comfortable. No wonder, centuries ago, the Spanish had forsaken Africa and turned their eyes westward to the Caribbean in their search for the land of gold: El Dorado. After them came the British, then the Dutch and French, exchanging what gold they found for more than its weight in blood, sweat and tears, much of it wrung from the bodies of slaves – human treasure from the 'dark continent' brought to harvest cane in the islands for the sweet tooth of European society. The Caribbean finds it difficult to forget its history.

On the appointed morning Barbados rose out of the dawn seascape, much as an old cinema organ appears at the intermission of some epic film, twinkling and sparkling in the half light with the tuneful promise of splendour and excitement to come.

This impression was made the more real by the cheerful music of Radio Barbados wafting round the chart-room from the headset of the radio direction finder, which I had tuned in to find a good landfall bearing. The lighthouse for which I had been hoping had failed to shine brightly enough for identification.

It was good to hear English spoken again, even if it was a little difficult to catch all the nuances of the strong West Indian accent. Closer to, the bright airport lights provided an excellent substitute for the dim lighthouse (which was operating, I discovered, on reduced power) and, right on track, we slid round South Point as the gong chimed for breakfast.

If we had come up on the island with the sun, so too had a trio of other small passenger ships – cruise liners whose regular, weekly visits were to become familiar to us during our stay. Spanish Main or Pirate Lake this sea may once have been, with galleons clouding the reefs. Now vessels on the island routes had Captain Morgan – on the bridge, in whites, not stomping a raging quarter-deck with parrot. And Don Juan or Senhor Fernando made his conquests to the thump of the disco beat, rather than the boom of calverine or rattle of musket. The only kick of the wheel to be felt was at the hands of the local taxi-drivers, completing an island tour in forty minutes flat (in case others were waiting for a similar breath-taking adventure back at the cruise liner quay).

Our graceful sister-ships formed a ragged queue off the single breakwater of Bridgetown deep-water harbour and waited, with us, for the pilot who commenced work at a civilized hour of the morning. Shortly after breakfast his launch came dancing out to us on the mirror-calm sea. One by one we were led inside.

Owing to the length of our visit, our berth was not on the passenger quays but across the harbour, at the grain wharf. This was used only occasionally by bulk cereal ships and was ideal for our purpose. It was accessible to the public, out of the port area, away from heavy traffic and, what was most important to us, right on the beach. So far on our journey we had grown used to taking long bus rides from the port area, wherever we had been berthed, to find safe running- and jumping-space for the children – and relaxation for ourselves. Having a beach on the doorstep was a Godsend. Two minutes walk if you ran, which môst of us did, it was there just for the asking at any time, and with the water calm and warm as a bath no opportunity was missed for a quick dash across the stony wharfside, under the grain hoppers, for a swift plunge.

The only drawback was the lurking sea urchin. These resolute, spiky guardians of the shoreline enjoyed the warm rocks and placid waters of the beach-front as much as we did, and watching where you put your feet was the only form of defence.

It was easy to fall in love with Barbados. If Brazil had dazzled us with its variety and size, Barbados stole our hearts with its warmth and simplicity. I have never been entirely happy about the description of Britain as a 'jewel, set in a silver sea'. But I have no reservations about such an accolade for this island, right down to its gold mounting of twenty-two carat sand.

The land is tear-shaped and emerald green with leafy vegetation – not two dozen miles long, north to south, and half of that across. Bridgetown, the capital, lies on the west side. This is the gentle, almost intimate coast. No great, wide, sweeping beaches here. Instead, short, homely stretches of sand, with dipping palms, the sea nudging lazily up to the shore, lapping and sinking absent-mindedly back, treating the land as it might a basking whale, accepted and caressed.

Houses, rich and poor together, edge down onto the sand and coconuts fall with a friendly thump on the coarse, bordering grass. Here, even nature is taking a break.

But over the central ridge of the island the eastern coast offers a wild and beautiful contrast. A broad swathe of beach, wide enough to stage a race meeting, runs for most of its length. This is broken occasionally by rocky promontories, as though specially placed for the stewards of the imaginary competition.

It is always the sea that one notices. Great, rolling breakers, carrying the full force of the southern ocean unhampered from the coast of Africa, slam heavily and unmercifully on this, the only obstacle in their path to the Americas. Booming and crashing, these high, curling waves surge up repeatedly against the innocent and unresisting shore, thudding down with a sensuous detonation, then hissing viciously back as a seething undertow.

Such is the weight and speed of the impact that a fine spray permanently mists the pulsating air over this furious junction of opposing elements. Beach guards are posted every few hundred yards to inform would-be swimmers of the exact location of the comparatively safe waters, where the rip is not too strong for wading.

A few yards either side of the beach guard's outstretched hand you would be swept off your feet, carried under and delivered as a warm breakfast to some passing shark or barracuda.

It is a thrilling coast. To hear, smell, see and feel the life of the sea and revel in its persistent assault on the land, sets the spirit surging with the waters. Through the kindness of a friend, Elizabeth and I were able to take the children for a weekend break in a simple cabin on this beach. Waking in the morning to the urgent beat of the surf outside and the rustle of a palm branch against the wooden shutters was an unforgettable experience.

One magical night the coarse scrub of a nearby dune caught light with a flickering necklace of fireflies. We woke the children and together crouched at the open casement watching, enchanted by their weaving, dipping dance. It was over in a moment – a shift of the breeze and they were blown onwards to a new ball-room, away across the coast road. But my memory of the heavy moon trailing its silver path shoreward, splintering into fragments at the surf-edge, the fireflies sparking on the sandy heath under its pale gaze, and the wide, shining eyes of my enraptured sons will remain with me for ever.

But we also loved Bridgetown. Even the name had a lighter touch than the solid Port Victorias and traditional Georgetowns that old British colonies of a certain size seem to attract as capitals. Bridgetown is a joyful and prosperous place, thanks in no small part to the tourists. It is small, but never quaint. The industry of the local people is too important. Even the small dock (the deep-water port is a little to the north of Bridgetown itself) which, of all places, might expect to be accused of quaintness, is altogether too practical – its island coasters loaded with crates of Coke, packs of T-shirts and tins of engine oil, its wharves bustling with minor commerce – to be much of a picturesque cameo.

It seemed very British to us, and we welcomed that after several months immersion in other cultures. Our subconscious selves were obviously thirsting for the reassuring touches of familiar 'home' things. But we were not severely afflicted. One pot of English jam and a packet of cereal, a treat for the children, filled the need.

If home was on *our* minds, it was even more on the minds of the majority of the crew. For we were about to lose two-thirds of them, around 200, who had come to the end of their commitment to the project.

For them, life aboard had started two years ago in Europe. They had traversed the Atlantic, circumnavigated South America and they had all grown, measurably, through the experience. Now the time had come to say goodbye and return home to their friends and families – in Europe, the Middle and Far East, Africa, North America . . . Initially they would take a charter flight to Belgium. Then, splitting up as a group like a bombarded atom, they would speed their way at random across the globe, taking with them the 'radiation' of their interaction to bring their understanding and Godly wisdom, by example, to their respective communities.

We ourselves were not going home, nor were most of the South American 'recruits' who had joined later. A few of the old hands would also be staying. Having been specially invited to take up responsible positions on board, perhaps, or feeling that they still had more to learn, they would have sought God's guidance, consulted with their parents at home, their friends, and church communities also, before signing on for a further voyage.

Oddly enough, those who did stay on in this way were often immediately put ashore, as part of a 'line-up' team. This was a group of half-a-dozen or so, led by a very experienced organizer, whose work was to go ahead of the ship, often months in advance, and prepare the way. They would contact officials, port authorities and church leaders, arrange clearances and obtain formal permissions, besides commencing the forest of paper-work that each visit entailed.

Although this was an adventurous and challenging task – the sharp end of the operation – it was also lonely and personally demanding, after the busy warmth of the shipboard community and much prayer was given and practical measures taken (including frequent, personal letters) to support these teams in the field.

But most would be leaving the ship for good, to be replaced by a similar number arriving fresh and new from as wide a source as the others. Part of the reason for our urgency in leaving Brazil was to arrive in time for the charter flight and the precise and complicated change-over this would involve.

All of us, naturally, viewed the loss of so many friends with sadness. We had known many only briefly. But those to whom the parting meant the break-up of rich friendships, forged in the oily heat of the engine-room or dusty cold of the dry store, the mountain roads of Chile or the swamplands of Maracaibo – twenty-four action-packed months – it was a youthful calamity.

These men and women had been labouring at the coal-face of world need, battling with seen and unseen forces, toiling and sharing together. One moment it would be over an intransigent essay for a tutor, the next an equally obstinate car tyre on a lonely, jungle road with night coming on and fifty miles still to go. Theirs was the friendship of veterans who have not only been baptized by fire, but have fought on through, in formal battle and local skirmish, attacking and withdrawing, deploying and re-grouping, binding up each others' wounds as opportunity arose, the campaign sweeping back and forth before their eyes.

It was no wonder, therefore, when the coaches arrived on the quayside under the brilliant glare of the Bajan sun, that a few soft tears were shed onto the weatherbeaten decks which had met so much salt water already, over the years.

For us there were some special farewells – to our family group. Each couple is assigned a number of singles as a sort of extended family. These we had come to know well: Ling-Cha, Dan, Gretta, Rinaldo, Louisa, Laars and Soshen. They had known us as 'father' and 'mother' – and for some this was no cute joke. Now they would be returning to their real families. It was strange to think that a part of us would be going to such different and unknown lands, in the shape of 'family' memories. If the impossible were to happen, and we were suddenly to arrive in a few weeks' time at the various addresses hastily written on the back of old envelopes now littering our cabin, it was strange to know that there would be a shout of welcome, an open door and a crowd of uncertain but smiling faces.

In what (to us) unspeakable, tortuous tongues would the details of Richard's first swimming-strokes or Timothy's smile be explained? Or our manner of taking a morning meeting and ability to organize a trip ashore be analysed and illustrated? Almost certainly we would not meet again this side of heaven. Unexpected thought.

Apart from all this, my ever-practical mind was dwelling also on the expert skills now tripping down from the forward gangways to the waiting coaches. Helmsmen, painters, lifeboatmen, riggers of gangways, slingers of books and vans – and that was only *my* department – all melting away like valuable water spilt on a desert floor. Hardened sailors all of them. And what were we getting in return? Bags of enthusiasm!

Well, I had been through it before. At least the feeling was not new. I had already prepared a short series of training lectures, at the mate's behest, though I knew as well as he did that most of the training would have to be done 'on the job'. The ship did not stop just because the crew had left. It would be 'business as usual' tomorrow, even if it was conducted a bit more slowly. That would apply all over the vessel: literature graduates would learn to stack books, motor mechanics to pump bilges, policemen to guide visitors to toilets and arts scholars to paint funnels – for *Doulos*, like the Spirit of God, is no respecter of persons when work is to be done. College Fellow or farm-hand, you worked where asked. Of course skills were not squandered, but a day together chipping rust in the cable locker made it easier to see that we were all equal before God – and to stow the anchor cable.

One evening, shortly before sailing, Elizabeth and I walked out along the shore near to the berth, a little way from the brightness and hum of the ship. The lights of Bridgetown winked across the harbour and the silver-tinged shoreline curved away sharply behind us. We sat down together on a rock. The sleepy sea smacked, hesitantly, close to our feet.

'Oh, darling, why can't we stay here for ever?' she whispered with a sigh. I watched the spiky black balls of the sea urchins jostle for position on the stony ledges, barely submerged under the transparent water. The daytime sun would drive them down deeper on the morrow.

'Islands are meant for coming and going, my love. It is their existence. Rather than wish to stay, we should resolve to come back one day.'

'We will, we will. One day. Oh, we must!'

16
And The Band Played On!

It took only a matter of hours to thread our way northward through the curved bow of the Windward Islands (Barbados is the tip of the arrow), tuck round to the south of St Croix and slip into the narrow Virgin Passage, to the East of Puerto Rico, our destination.

San Juan is the capital city of this large island – an exact rectangle, 100 miles by 50 – and reflects the American influence, almost colonial in feel, in the island as a whole. It is a big, broadly-spread metropolis, with wide multi-lane roads to take the familiar flat, brutish motor cars between the tall and graceless blocks of hotels or apartments.

We were fortunate to find a berth in the 'old town', which was the original Spanish settlement, and more attractive. This was the focus for the cruise ships and their sometimes ungentle cargo. The local people were most friendly. Though one could feel the violence of their nature, even through the genuine cordiality of our welcome – that passionate mixture of Spaniard and American which has made the Puerto Rican famed and feared on streets as far north as New York.

The streets of San Juan were not safe, either. During the first week of our stay, three of our number were held up – two at knife-point, losing their Bibles (which they ruefully hoped might at least do the criminal some good), and the last at the point of a gun.

Well, it would have been the point of a gun if the man in question, a cheerful and pragmatic Scot from the programme office, had not been so astounded at seeing done to him in real life what he had seen so often on television, that he merely laughed at the robber and walked on round the corner. It was when he returned to the ship that he started shaking. Just how close he had come to death was illustrated by the killing, not two months later (we heard from friends), of five American sailors in the same part of town because they, too, had refused the attentions of a roving gunman.

Old San Juan, which is now little more than a minor suburb of the main, modern city, had once been the capital of all the Spanish dominions in the Caribbean, and the military and naval headquarters of the Spanish Main.

From San Juan the Mexican treasure fleet, its holds bursting with Aztec gold, picked up its escort from the Imperial Navy for the Atlantic passage to Cadiz. From here, also, Spanish marines and musket regiments ventured abroad into the hinterlands of Colombia and Venezuela to find still more of the precious metal which they hoped would be lying around for the taking, and to plant the flag of His Most Catholic Majesty.

The truly massive fortress of El Morro, the most complex of its type in the whole of Latin America, illustrates this colonial importance. It dominates the entrance to the harbour and the cosy, quaint, Castilian town at its feet. Small streets cobble their way past shuttered windows and delicate wrought-ironwork from plaza to plaza, interlocking with the heavy bastions of the castle, above and below the walls.

The castle grounds were a wonderful place for the children to run and play, and we had particular success in flying kites, which took off and rode well in the brisk wind that whistled over the battlements, which were many feet thick in places.

In San Juan we attended our first Thanksgiving Dinner, invited by a local schoolmaster along with a few other families. Richard nearly made himself sick on the pumpkin pie, his father on the turkey. Thanksgiving is a unique and important day for Americans and we felt very honoured to be invited to share it with them.

The festive food put us in mind of Christmas, which was only weeks away. Our expected port for that day was Kingston, Jamaica, and from the reports we had received from the 'line-up' teams, any little presents we were aiming to buy had best be got before we sailed, for Jamaica was in the depths of an economic recesssion and there was little to purchase in any of the shops.

Accordingly all the local gift stores were amazed, having been used to the free-spending tourists from ships, to find hoards of people coming in asking for: 'Anything at around twenty cents please?' They had to rifle their old stock-cupboards and drawers to find any items that could possibly go at that price. Christmas would show how much ingenuity could make up for lack of regular funds.

But we nearly did not make it to Jamaica. In fact we nearly did not leave San Juan at all – and for once it had nothing to do with me.

As a precaution I had adopted the habit of watching the cruise liners leave when they were berthed astern of us. Very occasionally a rope gets caught or twisted from the other ship and a quick slackening or recovery of one's own line can save a lot of trouble and delay.

One evening it was the turn of a smart Cunarder. As usual with Cunard the last rope splashed into the water, without any snagging, exactly to the minute of the published time of departure.

I stood on our stern quarter and looked up at the lighted dance-floor (their stern was opposite ours), where couples were already beginning to savour the rhythm of a traditional Caribbean calypso. The tinkle of the music floated across on the back of an onshore breeze.

The harbour tugs took the strain and I raised my hand to the officer on her poop. His sailors were already packing the ropes down into their storage bins as her stern lifted from the quay. He threw a salute in reply. See you later, alligator. Sure thing, crocodile.

Gradually he moved away from me as the ship was drawn clear of the quay, plucked out of the line. If only cars could be made to do that, it would make parking so much easier. Then came a spurt of water from her counter, swirling its way forward along her water-line. She had put her engines astern to pull clear past us before letting the tugs spin her round for the entrance. She was over 100 yards off now, the bright line of her length slowly overlapping our own, moving further away all the time.

Or was she?

I noticed that the wash had stopped and she appeared to be stationary, almost exactly opposite our position. Not very wise, I thought, considering the wind, which was blowing quite stiffly onto the quay now. From her to us, in fact. I watched for the splash and ripple which would indicate she had resumed her manoeuvre. Perhaps she was going to turn where she was. She was well clear, anyway. But nothing happened.

The officer on her poop was engaged in frequent conversation on his radio, but no further motion came from the vessel herself, in fact, if anything, she was getting closer. I eyed the distance again. I'd be pushed to make it 100 yards now. More like eighty.

Surely she would kick her engines again? What were the tugs up to? They could hold her against the wind alone, but if she started drifting downwind? The momentum might be more difficult to arrest.

My heart gave a flutter of warning. Something was wrong. They should have acted by now.

The distance was down to sixty yards. There came a flurry of foam at her stern. I breathed a sigh of relief; she was pulling clear. Then her engines stopped. Having paused for a moment, she resumed her slow and menacing approach.

I realized with a shock that I would have to do something. Fenders! We would have to get some out. I looked anxiously along the length of the prom. deck. Two girls were leaning over the rail watching the liner, interested but unperturbed. That was all. They would be no help. They could not lift the heavy wickerwork over the side and lower it into place, even with my assistance. Mind you, I was not all that convinced of the ability of said items to protect us from the impact of 20,000 tons of floating hotel, shortly expected aboard.

Fifty yards. I turned and raced up the main staircase, two at a time, to the information office. Barging through the usual throng around the desk I grabbed the public address microphone and swung it towards me, slamming my fingers across the circuit switches. The startled girl behind stepped back sharply in surprise.

'Attention ship's company: control-party to the prom. deck foyer, right away! Control party to . . .' I repeated the announcement as I caught my breath. (The 'control-party' were the crew members trained and ready to fight fire on board.) The 'right-away' was unnecessary. I knew they would drop everything and come, anyway, but it was the most tactful way of telling the crew that this was no drill, without alarming the visitors.

I pushed aside the rather indignant crowd, once more, and ran back down to the deck, cannoning into the first arrivals of the control-party.

'Where's the fire? Why . . . ?'

I pointed to the approaching liner, now looming over us like a malevolent, dazzling starship from a distant galaxy, intent on our destruction.

'Fenders!' I gasped. All this exercise was bad for my health. 'Quick . . .'

Hastily I detailed the arriving men, some to collect fenders, others to find ropes to lower them down. The deck was transformed into a hive of activity, suddenly resembling, it seemed, the preparations for a naval battle.

Only twenty-five yards now separated the two vessels. On her upper deck the dance music faltered and died. A crowd of suddenly sober passengers had pressed themselves to the rail, drinks forgotten, party mood evaporating, watching the relentless meeting. On the poop, the lone officer stood rigid and helpless, gazing steadily down at our water-line. He spoke briefly and frequently into his walkie-talkie, counting down the distance.

We had three fenders over by now. Three squashy baskets the size of tractor tyres. Because of the special design of this class of Cunarders – they have a rounded waterline deck wider than the rest – I had requested them to be lowered to the water where she would hit first. I could see they were going to be about as useful as thistledown.

Suddenly a tug appeared around the Cunarder's stern.

Swinging round sharply, it inserted itself between us, put its nose up to her side and began to push, white water leaping from under its counter, a pale green in the fierce arc-lights. But the distance was too close, the angle too acute.

I saw a look of horror appear on the face of the tug captain as he realized the implication of his noble, but doomed, effort. If he did not pull out he would be crushed between the two steel hulls. Frantically the engine-room bells jangled on his small craft as he reversed his racing screws and backed clear of the closing jaws.

I nearly laughed, for the movement of his features had been so comical when he had seen the danger.

But our position was not so very different. Only one third the size of the descending vessel, with a concrete quay at our backs. I did not think we would be crushed, but the resulting damage might delay our departure for weeks, or even months.

The distance was down to feet only when I saw the officer on her poop move. He was shouting orders. I saw the high lights of a powerful ocean-going tug loom over the glass windbreak around her stern.

Maybe, just maybe, the cavalry had arrived. But they would have to be quick.

Wire ropes snaked out, his sailors running them quickly round the deck bollards.

Ten feet. I wanted to jump on board and help him out.

The wires on the poop twanged. Men jumped clear. He put his radio to his mouth. I lip-read his report: 'Tug fast, taking the weight.'

Six feet. They were not going to make it.

I looked at her angle and ordered another fender over the side, where I thought she would touch first. My mouth drew itself into a thin, grim line. My fingers tightened on the smooth, wooden rail.

But the blow never came.

Three feet clear, she stopped closing. We could have had drinks passed to us by the anxious tourists. The big tug had done her duty. Her powerful engines – titans that had hauled oil rigs across oceans and rescued supertankers – had been summoned to our aid too, in the nick of time. The jaunty stars-

143

and-stripes bobbing at her masthead in the stiff breeze showed that the cavalry had, indeed arrived.

The band struck up another number and the dancers returned to the floor.

We bent to recover our fenders.

Worse things happen at sea, I reflected, as I gave a hand with the ropes — even when you are still tied up to the shore.

You just never can tell.

17
Distinguished Visitors

'Ah! Just the man.'

I paused in my lunch-time task of injecting coloured pins into a chart of the Caribbean, which I had hung in the main foyer for the information of all and sundry, as we sailed towards Jamaica. A slight sense of foreboding crept over me.

'Would you mind popping into the office for a moment?'

I lifted an enquiring eyebrow at the programme manager, for it was he who had issued the invitation.

He wanted me to do something for him. That much was evident. Still, that was the general lot of all the workers in the programme office. If they were not typing or phoning, they were out scouring the decks, clip-board in hand, accosting groups of people with openers such as:

'How would you like to take part in . . . ?' Or: 'Actually we're a bit short on numbers for . . .' Or even, with a pleading look: 'I just don't know how we are going to . . . unless (eyes lighting up) *you* might consider . . ?'

After a few weeks of this, any one of them could have sold ice cream to Eskimos or double glazing to Bedouins, with their hands tied behind their backs. It was not that we were reluctant to help them out, it was just that there was so much else to do.

I seem to have heard that excuse before.

As for me, I could see my number was up, whatever he had in mind. I was about to receive the full attention of the Top Man, alone in his office. An away match. It was all over, I hadn't a chance. I decided to go quietly.

'Sure, I've got a few minutes, I think.' I glanced pointedly at my watch. Maybe I could keep the talk on generalizations for a bit and then suddenly notice the time. I should hope. I told you: this guy was a master. No sooner had the door closed than he came out with it.

145

'Clive, we were wondering if you would consider taking over as Master of Ceremonies for the "Opening" receptions in future.'

I started to return the volley with something suitable like: 'Oh, were you now?' when he cut me off with a forehand smash down the centre line.

'No! Please. Don't give me your answer right away. I know you are a busy man . . .' He opened the door. 'Thanks for dropping by.'

I left, at least two sets down on the first serve. The minute-hand on my watch hadn't even budged. I didn't know it was possible. Absent-mindedly I picked up a pin and stuck it in our noon position, measuring the co-ordinates by eye. Landfall tomorrow afternoon. Somehow the prospect did not seem quite as attractive, after all.

I thought about it. But I gave no answer that day, waiting until the following, when the Blue Mountains of the eastern uplands were hanging close over our starboard side as we worked our way along the south-east coast towards Kingston. I did not intentionally keep him waiting. Not really. It was something I had to consider carefully.

Every port we visited, the line-up teams would issue invitations prior to our arrival, from the captain to various dignitaries and senior members of the local community. These were to attend a special reception on board held at the commencement of our stay and timed to coincide with the official opening of the book exhibition in that port. A distinguished guest would top the list and be invited to cut the ribbon at the conclusion. Over the years we have received national presidents, cabinet ministers, city mayors and church leaders in this capacity. Even since our return to the ship we had seen state governors, port admirals and ambassadors wrestle with scissors and tape.

The reception itself would consist of soft drinks and cake (the latter had, of course, always ensured my attendance in the past), a short introduction by the director, some songs from the singing-group, who were inclined to humour as well as choral excellence, a slide show on the work of the ship and the presentation of a small gift. This was nearly always a few books, including our bestseller – the Bible.

The meeting was concluded by a speech, hopefully short, from the distinguished guest and then an ascent to the boat-deck where the ribbon awaited. It was the closest we ever got to formal public relations. Important people were being introduced to the ship for the first time and their impressions would colour many people's judgement of our efforts. Invariably there was a Press presence and normally television in addition. A lot hung on this. And I was being asked to run it.

The MC greeted the guests and escorted the distinguished visitor, made polite conversation (with translation, if required) announced the songs, the slide presentation, the ship director, filled the gap when the projector bulb failed, the guitars needed tuning or the TV cameras were late, arranged for the rescue of presidential aides who fell down gangways, scissors that went missing or wigs that went awry. In short, the MC was the lynch-pin of the occasion.

Up until now the task had been ably performed by one who had had considerable experience of the organization, ashore and afloat, moved and spoke like oiled butter and would have convinced the honoured guests, had the ship sunk under them, that this was an entirely normal part of the day and he would be delighted to show them a lifeboat on their way out. But he had left and, although I was not in the same league, the ball had landed as they say, in my court.

I was lying comfortably in my hammock, slung in a corner of the prom. deck, watching the land slide by, when the head of the programme manager rose like an inquiring moon over the tasselled foot of my full-sized cradle.

'Well?' he said. Underrated this man, for his ability to communicate.

'Who's the guest?' I countered.

'Oh, didn't I tell you? The Governor-General.'

'Ah . . . right,' I replied calmly, steadying the unexpected motion of the hammock with my outstretched arm. The ship had not moved.

'Pop round to my office for a briefing tomorrow, then?'

'Er . . . OK.'

'Good.'

His face set quickly over the woolly curve of my horizon. Game, set and match. I'd got the job.

The first aspect of Kingston harbour hove into view. Most of us, in fact, were looking forward to Jamaica with a mixture of excitement and concern. We had been told that the island had suffered severely in recent years from the effects of a trade recession and, in consequence, there was very little to buy in the shops and open violence on the streets – certainly of Kingston, if not some of the smaller towns.

So concerned had the authorities become for our safety that they had arranged for the ship to have a continuous armed guard of twelve policemen, on duty night and day, for our protection. Although this news made us all rather wary, it did show an active interest on behalf of the government in the purpose of our visit. They were delighted we had chosen the, rather depressed, capital for our base, in preference to the more prestigious areas of Montego Bay, 100 miles to the north-west, on the tourist coast.

Kingston was where the need was, in their opinion and in ours, but it was also where we would be most at risk. In the event we had no trouble at all. Threats, yes, against individuals and the ship. But nothing materialized. With our squad of policemen, and taking the sensible precaution of raising our gangways at night, we stayed secure.

In fact, we reaped an odd benefit from the troubles (now, thankfully, largely over) in that the nearby Intercontinental Hotel which was nearly empty of guests, offered the crew free use of their swimming-pool. It was a most generous gesture and thanks to their kindness I am proud to report that Richard, aged four, first learnt to swim in a first class hotel pool in the Caribbean. The only one to disapprove was Timothy, who felt that 'bombing' people as they swam past (including his struggling brother) to the accompaniment of bloodcurdling screams, was a more valid way of enjoying the facility.

The reception was scheduled for forty-eight hours after our

berthing. I searched out my formal, white uniform and gave orders to the staff to have it cleaned and pressed. Elizabeth patiently complied.

I made notes on everything: who was coming, what I would say, what they would say, what the captain would say, what was to be sung, etc., etc. I drew a line at noting my own name, but only just.

All this, not much larger in size than a modest history of the world, I secreted inside my uniform cap. A quick glance down into my doffed headgear and any hesitation could immediately be covered by recourse to the facts. (This actually worked so well that I adopted it for all consequent receptions, until the day came when I had to introduce the Bahamian Prime Minister and found I had left my hat outside – but that is another story.)

I also wandered around the main lounge, checking the slide projector and microphones. Here I was curtly informed that one does not exhale violently all over a delicate instrument in order to test it, and how would I like someone to come up and blow all over my sextant? So I wandered outside to look at the (temporary) VIP gangway.

'You can't expect the representative of Her Majesty the Queen to clamber up that filthy heap of ironmongery!' I commented, tactfully, to the mate, as I found him supervising the rigging of the accommodation ladder for the purpose.

'What it needs is a good scrub and some canvas screens down the side.'

'Soap we have, screens we have, wall-to-wall sailors we haven't,' he replied, carefully studying the architecture of the waterfront buildings.

'All right, where's the gear?' I sighed eventually, after a long pause. I could see I would have to do it myself. In the event, Enrico the fireman gave me a hand and, like a couple of agitated charwomen, we set to with scrubber, mop and bucket. The mate later relented and sent a man down with the screens and we lashed them taut, top and bottom. In the end it looked very smart. Fit even for the Queen herself, should she have been passing through.

After lunch, I changed into my crackling 'ice cream' suit and walked stiffly down to my station on the quayside, my hat balancing delicately on my head, owing to the three-volume script stuffed within. The programme office assistant followed on.

At the top and bottom of the sparkling gangway stood other officers in similar white attire, while inside in the lounge ante-room waited the ship director, captain and others in a 'welcome line'.

Already guests were arriving and we indicated the gangway, handing them on up the chain which ended with a glass of lemon juice in one hand and a piece of cake in the other and conversation with a nervous crew member in the lounge. My companion indicated that the hour had come. Along the street motor-cycle outriders turned the corner, followed by a long, black limousine. I noted that it had a crown instead of a number plate. The Governor-General was approaching. Smoothly the car drew onto the quayside and stopped, the motor-cyclists dismounted. A military aide leapt out of the front and swung open the door.

I saluted in time with the others as the man himself emerged. He stood up and stretched out his hand with a smile.

'Welcome to Jamaica,' he said. I felt that he meant it.

We walked together to the accommodation ladder and cameras clicked as we climbed the side into the cool interior. He paused to shake hands with all the officers on his route, renewing his greeting to everyone. I fed him and his entourage into the welcome line and skipped round to ensure that a seat and juice awaited him in his reserved corner of the ante-room.

If everything was going to run as smoothly as this, I thought, I was going to enjoy myself. Unexpectedly, that is just what happened. The presentation in the main body of the lounge ran on automatic. I forgot nothing that my notes could not supply and the Governor-General rounded off proceedings with a witty (and brief) speech, wishing us every blessing in our endeavours. He cut the ribbon and cleared the side in under two, very pleasant, hours with nary a hitch. It was considered a great success.

'Oh Clive, you were wonderful,' enthused Elizabeth, after the excitement had died down and the captains and Queen's representative had departed, and fires were sinking on most of the dunes and headlands in sight.

''Course, I put it down to the uniform, myself,' she added, not wishing to inflate my conceit much beyond bursting-point.

'I see your point, my love,' I replied thoughtfully. 'It certainly would have been difficult to sound as confident if I hadn't been wearing anything . . .'

I dodged to avoid the aerial passage of my uniform cap, which spun across the cabin towards me, shedding guiding notes, like overweight confetti, en route. But if I managed to avoid the missile, I had reckoned without the prime mover, who followed in hot pursuit. I had less objection to that impact.

18
Christmas — And Home

Christmas Eve had arrived and, throughout the vessel, decorations had appeared to prove it. In the main lounge a Christmas tree had taken root. Along all the corridors and down companionways paper greenery vied with silver and red tinsel or home-made holly and berries.

Cabin doors were decorated with individual items, illustrating the traditional celebrations of their occupants, many of them used to the warmer climate for the festival. These showed the imagination and ingenuity of the crew at its best, being for the most part made from simple card, coloured paper and whatever could be scrounged from friends and neighbours by way of cloth, ribbon or old gift-wrapping.

Used greetings cards were cut out and pasted up into new ones, which, with the addition of skilful drawing, often improved on the original, in our estimation. It certainly made the exchange of cards a very personal activity.

Elizabeth and I prepared for Christmas Day in the knowledge that our (new) family group would be coming round to our cabin for the morning, to share in the opening of presents. Each had arranged to buy or make something for just one of the others, having chosen 'lots' some weeks before, and we looked forward to some fond and perhaps wistful, recollections of Christmas at home from each of them. Elizabeth would prepare some special fare and we would re-create something of the festival we were all used to, in different forms. A family occasion in a foreign land.

There would be some very mixed feelings in the group. They were only a matter of weeks into the two years of their service and very far from home. This time last year, they had probably had little inkling of the step they were about to make. They had little knowledge of the strange, moving home to which they were now committed. They would be feeling the first bite of regret at this, very personal, time of the year – the first realization of the magnitude of the task they had taken on; the first pains of the sacrifice.

We knew. We had been there, too. For, as we looked back over all our trials and triumphs, we saw that it had been a difficult path to follow, an unusual and 'unworldly' choice to make. We had been asked to pay more than we had wanted, work harder than we had wished, give more of ourselves than we had ever given before. We also knew that this was exactly what God had intended.

At Christmas, with the new, unknown, exciting year stretching ahead and the old filled with so many events and memories, lying behind, we knew we would be needed to encourage and advise, remember and re-live, enquire and listen for the benefit of our new friends and family. It was a new beginning, another end.

On Christmas Eve itself lunch was devoted to the poor of the Kingston area. Several hundred of the most destitute came aboard for this strangely-moving event and all of us took turns at serving the tables in the dining saloon with the simple chicken and potatoes that had been prepared. For those who came it was a feast fit for a King.

It is difficult to describe how those poor, lined faces lit up at the sight of food; how they responded to a little love. The patience with which they waited for their meal to arrive; the pleasure on their features as they plunged into their own, private, individual portion; the grateful smile as they finished their plates, bloated on a modest meal. It was a small gesture, perhaps. It did not attack the roots of their poverty. But I was sure they would not forget it, nevertheless.

More than one server from the crew had to retire to weep a little at the gentle, but poignant emotion in the air.

I had been asked to speak at the end of the meal. As I stood up, they immediately grew silent in quiet attention. I took confidence from their genuine interest and spoke of the many things that God had provided for the ship and her crew.

I spoke of the different countries we had visited, the many

people we had met on our travels, and of the reason why we did it. I spoke of Christmas and of the Prince of Peace, whose birthday it was, of the Wonderful Counsellor whose advice we sought and followed from the pages of the Bible, which we carried all over the world, of the Everlasting Father whose concern was always for our highest good, of the Mighty God whose power was at our backs and whose promises were our pathway through the conflicts and confusions of the present times.

'If,' I concluded, 'there is any hope in the world that we can live fuller and better lives, any hope that man can ever look his fellow man in the face and call him brother – and mean it – any hope that truth, honour and justice will eventually prevail, then I believe it can be found only in the forging of a relationship with God himself, through the link that Jesus Christ provides.

'Look around, feel the table, the deck under your feet, see the walls and windows across the room. Feel your stomachs. None of these things have been provided by us, though people are involved in all of them. Not one of us here, with all our skills, is capable of running a ship of this size and complexity without outside help. I know. I know because I have worked on ships for the whole of my adult life. God moves and grants us that help.'

I sat down. I had said enough.

Slowly, hesitantly, from across the room came the clap of a single pair of hands. Then came another, followed by another and another. Like a flooding torrent the applause rose up and echoed around the saloon, spilling out of the doorway, up the stairs and out onto the deck above.

For a moment I looked around, embarrassed. Then I realized they were not clapping me.

Unobtrusively, silently, I added my applause to theirs.

'*Doulos, Doulos*, this is Nassau Port Control, over.'

'*Doulos, Doulos*, Motor Vessel *Doulos*, this is Nassau Port Control. How do you read – channel eight, over?'

The insistent warble of the VHF radio in the wheel-house

broke in upon my wandering thoughts, cutting off the flow of reminiscence. I noticed that Jeff had left my side to attend to the communication. I had been, truly, miles away. I followed him into the shadowed interior to catch the gist of the message.

'Hello Port Control, this is *Doulos*, over.'

'*Doulos*, Port Control, sorry but your berth will not be available until two o'clock, over.'

I took the handset from Jeff and replied.

'*Doulos* roger, please reschedule our pilot for thirteen forty-five, over.'

'Ah, will do, sir. Port Control out.'

I returned the handset.

'I'll tell the captain,' I volunteered. Uncommitted to the anchor watch, it was time I went below and got on with some other work. I would pass his cabin on my way.

'OK, see you.' Jeff lifted his hand in acknowledgement and returned to the outside rail, to resume his interrupted thoughts. I slid down the ladder to the captain's deck. My mind ran on also for a moment or two — back to Jamaica and the spectacular, floodlit sail from Kingston; the raging storm which followed; the gracious food and live entertainment offered to the whole ship's company in the Palace of Culture in Vera Cruz, Mexico; the unforgettable saga of the Coatza Water Board (who had lots of water but nothing to put it in); Mardi Gras; the admiral who moved five warships to let us have the berth we wanted . . . so much had happened. With a further effort of will, I returned to the present.

I knocked at the captain's door.

'Come in, come in Clive, take a seat. What can I do for you?' I explained the change of time. I have known captains to be violently angry at a delay of minutes, let alone hours. But I knew he would not be. He threw up his hand in a dismissive gesture.

'Ah, what does it matter? The Lord knows why we've gotta wait, eh, Clive? And that's the truth.'

I nodded in agreement. I could do little else, for I knew he was right. I had seen God in action too many times and in too many ways by now to doubt the truth of the captain's words.

Often I had understood little of the way he had worked and seen only a partial reason for events, but I had seen enough to convince me he was there.

'Where're you going when you leave? Anything planned?' the captain continued, picking up the train of thought which had started, unbeknown to him, somewhat earlier on the deck above.

'Ah, yes, sir. Home first and settle back into our little cottage on the hill in Kent, I think. After that, well . . .' I glanced up at his interested and rather concerned countenance across the cabin. 'After that is in the Lord's hands, isn't it, sir?'

His craggy features cracked into a broad smile.

'That's right, Clive, that's just about right, and don't you forget it!' He gestured around him as he spoke, taking in the whole of the ship with a sweep of his hand – the hum of machinery, the excited chatter on the deck outside, the distant chuckle of the small wavelets against our anchored hull.

'He's never forgotten *us*, now, has he?'